SHOWCASE OF INTERIOR DESIGN™

Eastern Edition II

Vitae Publishing, Inc.
Grand Rapids, MI

Published in the United States
by Vitae Publishing, Inc.
50 Monroe Avenue NW
Suite 400
Grand Rapids, MI 49503
800-284-8232

Library of Congress
Cataloging-in-Publication Data

Showcase of Interior Design, Eastern Edition II
p. cm.
Includes indexes.
ISBN 1-883065-01-1 (hard)
1-883065-02-x (soft)
1. Interior decoration-Eastern States-History-20th Century.
I. Mary Jane Pool
NK2004.S55 1994 729'.025'74 - - dc20 94-2452 CIP

VITAE PUBLISHING, INC.

CHAIRMAN - JOHN C. AVES
PRESIDENT - JAMES C. MARKLE
VICE PRESIDENT - GREGORY J. DEKKER

EASTERN EDITION PRODUCTION STAFF

Communication Manager - Christine A. Humes
Editor - Nancy White Bryant
Editor - Maria C. Cutler
Editor - Gita M. Gidwani
Editor - Jennifer Crier Johnston
Editor - Majda Kallab
Editor - Francine E. Port
Contributing Author - Mary Jane Pool

AVES, INCORPORATED

Production Artist - Nancy J. Allen
Production Operations Manager - Douglas Koster
Copy Editor - David Knorr
Client Services Manager - Carolyn Zank
Financial Management - Jeanne Seaman and Kathleen D. Kelly

Printed in Singapore by Toppan
Typeset in USA by Vitae Publishing, Inc.

Title Page Interior Design Firm: Pedro Rodriguez Interiors:
Photographer: Barry Halkin

Providing an elegant background for an eclectic art collection
was the primary concern in designing this living room.
Details such as the sculptured carpeting help visually shorten
the long, narrow space.

Prologue

*Y*ou are invited to enjoy, study, emulate and acquire the ideas and talents in this cornucopia. Our mission is to build a bridge from a premier resource of professional interior design talent over the river of uncertainty and into a reader's home.* Showcase of Interior Design *has reached 100,000 homes with books like the one in your hands, but we only communicate with one reader at a time. Our task is personal. The selection of styles, cost, location and personalities is very eclectic. One of our goals is to be as inclusive as possible, offering readers the opportunity to find a comfortable fit with their own concept of home. The qualifications of each designer are presented so that their level of professionalism can be evaluated objectively by our readers.*

Enjoy the richness and variety of over 200 stimulating photographic examples of leading edge interior design. Study the use of color, volume, detail and space. Emulate, if you wish, the acknowledged masters.

After you have absorbed the fun and education in Showcase of Interior Design, *we hope you will acquire some of this talent directly. Invite one or more of these fine professionals to help you sculpt and weave and paint your own personal expression of home.*

John C. Aves

Table Of Contents

BELOW: Juan Montoya:
Wood paneling is reflected in the mirror, creating a seemingly transparent "curtain-like" separation between the entry and the living room.

Would The Ideal Interior Designer Consider You An Ideal Client?

By Mary Jane Pool

To reach the elevated status of "ideal client" is not difficult if you do some advanced thinking and talking about what you expect of the space you call home. When you have some idea of how you want your rooms to perform – the use, or the look, or the feel – it is time to call in an expert to complete the picture.

A favorite client of the legendary designer Billy Baldwin wrote wonderful letters that he said "described not how she wanted things to look, but how she wanted things to feel." For instance: "If you had been out all day and knew I was waiting at home in some silky dressing gown, what kind of mood would you be in? Do you expect your interest in me to be quenched by a lot of cold high-fashioned atmosphere ... Do you realize that it matters very much how a chair feels when you sit in it? Do you realize that you are extravagantly crazy about luxury?"

Although she was writing to Billy, he knew she was talking to her husband. Billy got the message immediately. It was clear she wanted comfort and come-hither, not hard-edge, show-stopping spectacular. Their association was a great success and lasted for years.

You may have some definite ideas

OPPOSITE: Pedro Rodriguez Interiors: The designer conserved space in this relatively small multipurpose room by using a projection T.V. The screen peeks down from the ceiling above the faux travertine fireplace surround.

about how you want your space to look. Recently, I read about a young magazine editor who planned the redecoration of his apartment meticulously. It was reported: "He tore out pictures of things he liked and hated from magazines and bound them together in a book for his decorator. He included his own Ten Commandments of Good Taste. (For example: 'Avoid Regency wallpaper.''Dismiss the fifties.''Sisal is the enemy.')" Talking about what you dislike can be just as helpful as talking about what you like. Your designer will be grateful for your frankness. It will help to put you on the same wavelength and make you a good working team.

And "working team" it should be. Designer Albert Hadley says he does his best work for clients who "understand the creative process and become part of it." He describes several as "energetic, educated, passionate about their clothes and homes and, most importantly, open-minded." In other words, "not an empty canvas."

In his book, "Billy Baldwin Remembers," Billy writes about a creative effort for the client who wrote the "wonderful letters." Here is how he describes the creation of the living room in their city apartment: "The owners wanted colors that would keep the room in the sky; so, of course, it is blue and white, which is what the heavens are made of. To give the room a solid footing on a cloud, I paved the floor with

BELOW: Kenneth Hockin Interior Decoration Inc.: Wool Tartan draperies, an antique Charles X mirror over the mantel, and a mahogany Victorian leather-topped partner's desk highlight this library. The colors were inspired by the antique Oriental carpet.

squares of white vinyl, then found the clue to the whole decorating scheme, a ravishing blue-and-white antique Indian durrie rug for a magical Tunisian look.

"I was going mad trying to find exactly the right furniture for this magic-carpet room, so I designed it myself: banquettes and chairs with Turkish pantaloon skirts. The blue chair covering is rough raw silk, a sort of regal denim. The banquettes are covered with wall fabric, a creamy grège textured cotton, nice to touch. The pillows look like silk brocade but they aren't. They're linen and cotton.

"We already had the immensely decorative Indian-wood and ivory mirror to hang over the fireplace, but I was desperate about the mantel. Some conventional French thing just wouldn't do. I asked one of my partners, Arthur Smith, to design the mantel, and he came up with a perfect one – polished steel and mirror. Now, I thought, what this room needs is something eccentric, something astounding. By sheer luck, I found it: a pair of tall painted-wood Mogul finials carved as intricately as lace – finials as old, maybe, as Akbar. The result is perfection: the great new, the great old."

Contemporary paintings and tables of recent design add more of the new to this setting. A wall of windows fills the room with sunshine, and modern lighting makes it shimmer at night. It suits very well the working couple who want to step into another world when they come home from the office. It is a room that is comfortable, full of fantasy and refreshing to the senses.

Like any work of art, a successful room is the result of an unfolding process. A need is born, a scene is set, an atmosphere evolves. When client and designer see eye-to-eye, it is "ideal." And when the creative sparks begin to fly, an exciting, rewarding experience is just ahead.

Mary Jane Pool, an editor of *Vogue* Magazine and editor-in-chief of *House & Garden* 1970-1980, is a consultant to the Baker Furniture Company and Aves, Inc. She edited *Billy Baldwin Decorates* and *20th Century Decorating, Architecture and Gardens.* She is co-author of *The Angel Tree, A Christmas Celebration*, a book about the 18th Century Creche Collection at the Metropolitan Museum of Art, published by Harry N. Abrams; and *The Gardens of Venice* and *The Gardens of Florence* published by Rizzoli. She serves on several boards including the Decorative Arts Trust and The Isabel O'Neil Foundation for the Art of the Painted Finish.

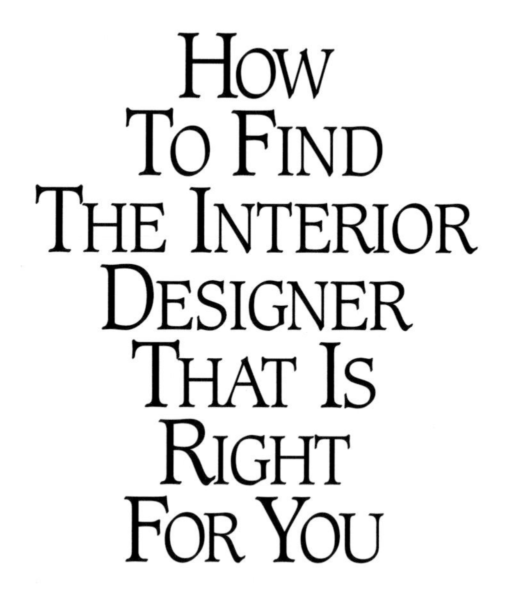

How To Find The Interior Designer That Is Right For You

Buying this book means you have a point of view about decoration and design, and the makings of an "ideal client." As you go through the pages, you will sample the work of a number of well-qualified interior designers. It is a unique way to see and compare some of the country's great design talents.

When you find rooms that appeal to you, call the designer, or designers, for an appointment. Ask each one to visit you to see the things you like to live with, or perhaps a way of life you want to discard. Do your

BELOW: Pedro Rodriguez Interiors: In this informal entertaining area, artwork reflects the client's devotion to her garden. Neutral furniture heightens interest in the colorful accents. Bare windows allow the surrounding gardens to become part of the interior.

OPPOSITE: Shields & Company: A curved marble and oak fireplace is the central architectural detail from which a living room, sunroom and dining room fan out.

ABOVE: Billy W. Francis Design/Decoration, Inc.: This intimate dining space with a view of Central Park is perfect for small gatherings.

OPPOSITE: Donald A. Rich Interiors & Antiques: An antique Chinese screen dominates a wall in this narrow room and helps tie the various elements together.

homework. Be prepared to talk about the design project you have in mind in some detail, including your budget and timing. The designers will be able to respond more quickly and efficiently, and tell you right away if what needs to be done will fit into your time frame. From these initial meetings, you will be able to narrow the field, or even make your final choice.

Discuss the business procedures of the design firm. Does the designer charge a one-time fee, hourly consultation fees, retail markups, percentages on construction? Does the designer present estimates with a request for a deposit? For instance, some designers prefer to estimate and bill for each purchase, asking for a 50 percent deposit before placing orders. Others bill by the month or by the project.

How will you work together on floor plans and color schemes? Will the designer present a drawing of how a room is envisioned, complete with swatches of materials and photographs of suggested furnishings?

Visit the designer's office and see work completed for other clients. When you have chosen the designer you think is right for you, exchange credit references and letters confirming how you will work together. What is best for designer and client should be decided in advance to make the project unfold smoothly.

Developing an environment that suits your needs and moods, indeed, is a creative process. One that has a beginning and, ideally, never an ending. The space you call home should periodically be updated and refreshed to keep up with you and your times. Through the pages of this *Showcase* book, you will find an interior designer who will consider you a treasured, ideal client. A designer you can turn to with the greatest pleasure and confidence, knowing the result of your collaboration will give you and your family just what you want – perhaps even a dream come true.

Antine Associates Inc

ANTHONY ANTINE
1028 ARCADIAN WAY
PALISADE, NJ 07024
(201)224-0315 FAX(201)224-5963

200 EAST 77TH STREET
NEW YORK, NY 10021
(212)988-4096

Antine Associates Inc

PUBLISHED IN:
Interior Design
House Beautiful
The New York Times
British HG
Colonial Home
Woman's Wear Daily
Design Times
Country Life
New Jersey Monthly
100-Designers Favorite Rooms
Showcase of Interior Design, 1991, 1993
Beyond The Bath
Beyond The Kitchen
Media Design
The New York Daily News
The Washington Post
Various other publications

PROJECTS:
Private Residences: in the United States; England; Korea; Japan and Italy.

Commercial Work: The Point Hotel, Saranac Lake, New York; Residential models and lobbies for Hartz Mountain Industries and the Punia Company; Lake Placid Lodge in Lake Placid.

CREDENTIALS:
Education F.I.T.
ISID, Served as Vice President and Board Member
Representative to IDLYNY
Kips Bay Boys and Girls Club Showhouse 1994
Barron's Who's Who, 1990, 1991, 1992, 1993
Rogers Memorial Library Southhampton Showhouse 1993, 1994
Saratoga Showhouse in conjunction with the New York State Museum 1993

APPEARANCES:
Good Morning New York
Today Show
CNN "Style"

Clara Hayes Barrett Designs

CLARA HAYES BARRETT
300 BOYLSTON STREET
BOSTON, MA 02116
(617)749-5876 FAX (617)426-6415

Private Residences: New York; Florida; Nantucket, Massachusetts; Connecticut; Vermont; New Hampshire; Virginia and South Carolina.

Commercial Work: Stonehill College; Carlton House Condominiums; South Boston Savings Bank and Hyatt Hotel.

CREDENTIALS:
Ladycliffe College
Stonehill College
Rhode Island School of Design

PUBLISHED IN:
House Beautiful
Traditional Home
House & Garden
Decorating
Metropolitan Home
Design Times
Boston Magazine

OPPOSITE: Varied aesthetic traditions exist together in this living room. The contrasting themes of simplicity and luxury are evident in the antique Persian carpet and the finest fabrics and upholstery.

ABOVE: Sunlight streams into this Nantucket living room through the silk draperies and crystal beading. The 18th century American portrait and antique Swedish chest add traditional grace.

BELOW: Pastels suffuse this Back Bay bedroom with good cheer. Family treasures and a painted ceiling add to the warmth. The bed is adorned with an antique quilt and lace.

OPPOSITE: A traditional grace pervades this guest bedroom. Delicate tambour canopies the bed, and roses "bloom" on the headboard and dust ruffle.

H.R. Beckman Design

HESTER R. BECKMAN
3600 CONSHOHOCKEN AVENUE
PHILADELPHIA, PA 19131
(215)473-2106

PROJECTS:
Private Residences: New Jersey; Florida; New York; Pennsylvania and numerous show houses.

Commercial Work: Banks, medical offices, organizational offices, meeting rooms and backdrops for citywide events.

CREDENTIALS:
Philadelphia College of Art, A.D.
Temple University, B.S., J.D.
University of Pennsylvania, M.S.
Special training in architecture, computer design, lighting and display

PUBLISHED IN:
New York Times
Philadelphia Inquirer
Philadelphia Bulletin
Sacramento Union
Miami Herald
Evening Phoenix
Who's Who In The East

BELOW: Client art, a magnificent lacquer and glass coffee table and ultrasuede swivel chairs, in subtle colors, compliment the magnificent view.

PHILOSOPHY:
Widely traveled, with an architectural background, I emphasize comfort, convenience and drama, tempered by restraint.

No particular era has a monopoly on beauty, I add inconspicuous technology to yesterday or subtle elegance to tomorrow.

Your possessions, inherited or collected, express your individuality. My designs reflect the client, not the designer.

Your home, your refuge and your castle, should send you forth each day sufficiently refreshed to face any challenge - to lift your wings and soar.

BELOW: Of Beckman design, the furniture emphasizes beauty and convenience. Curved to follow the sofa and facing the Intercoastal Waterway, a Lucite and laminate desk doubles as breakfast table. The wall unit contains T.V., Hi-Fi, bar and storage.

H.R.
BECKMAN
DESIGN

BELOW: Illuminated from outside, day and night, stained glass displaces a wall of closets. A portion of the edge-lit steps are movable for plumbing access.

RIGHT: Custom built cherry cabinetry houses basins, refrigerator, hamper and linen storage. A floor-to-ceiling mirror, etched to match the wallpaper, conceals the toilet and bidet.

BELOW OPPOSITE: Tranquility and additional storage space were the prime objectives. The base of each Beckman designed lamp is of semiprecious rock.

ABOVE LEFT: The carved glass panel, edge-lit with neon, forms a corridor to the bath and dressing rooms. The angled Beckman designed headboard conceals an integral, corridor accessed chest of drawers.

ABOVE RIGHT: This small under-the-eaves bath provides privacy for two by means of a pocket door. The bronze mirror divider walls contain spherical fish tanks.

ABOVE: In a large, formerly unused, room dreams are realized. A mirror wall conceals patio access, its Lucite projection provides a recirculating waterfall. Behind sliding doors are a small refrigerator, TV Hi-Fi, clothing and linen storage. Unseen are a sauna, shower, toilet, bidet, vanity, exercise equipment and art.

William Beson Interior Design, Ltd.

WILLIAM BESON, ASID, ALLIED MEMBER
WILLIAM BESON INTERIOR DESIGN, LTD.
INTERNATIONAL MARKET SQUARE
275 MARKET STREET, SUITE 530
MINNEAPOLIS, MN 55405
(612)338-8187 FAX (612)338-2462

RENÉE LEJEUNE HALLBERG, ASID,
ALLIED MEMBER

Photographer: Lark Gilmer

PROJECTS:
Private Residences: Minneapolis and St. Paul, Minnesota; Aspen and Denver, Colorado; Palm Desert, California; Naples and Port Royal, Florida and Washington, D.C.

Commercial Work: Executive offices, law firms and hospitality

CREDENTIALS:
William Beson:
ASID, Allied Member
"Star on the Horizon" Award, Chicago Design Sources

Renée LeJeune Hallberg:
ASID, Allied Member

PUBLISHED IN:
Numerous national and local publications

OPPOSITE: Faux marble walls create an excellent background for opulent detail. The warm color palette contributes to the welcoming ambiance.

LEFT: The evident attention to detail reflects the integrity of our design excellence.

BELOW: A blending of periods and styles supports the use of varied patterns to create a feeling of sophisticated elegance.

PHILOSOPHY:
Our designers interpret the client's needs both practically and aesthetically to create the ideal environment. We pride ourselves on the versatility of our styles which enables us to work with clients from a contemporary "less is more" attitude to the lavish traditional interiors shown here. Our impeccable style is coupled with top notch service and a sense of integrity which constantly drive us to strive for the very best.

JOSE SOLIS BETANCOURT
1751 N STREET NW
WASHINGTON, D.C. 20036
(202)659-8734 (212)465-1973

PHILOSOPHY:
I take an academic approach to integrating architecture and interiors. My goal is to achieve function and comfort by means of proportion and harmony.

Prior to forming Solis Betancourt, I trained as an architect at Cornell University and gained years of experience in the offices of Skidmore, Owins and Merrill, as well as the office of John F. Saladino. Solis Betancourt has accepted numerous award-winning commissions.

BELOW: The offices of an investment firm provide residential elegance and comfort without sacrificing efficiency and durability.

OPPOSITE: A Washington, D.C., breakfast room features an extraordinary collection of ancient Greek vases on illuminated display stands, designed by Solis Betancourt.

OPPOSITE ABOVE LEFT: A Jacobean Style Library where soft pleated sheers drape across Solis Betancourt's Mediaeval inspired wall sconces. Custom seating and upholstery are integrated with museum quality antiques to provide Betancourt's trademark "Casual Elegance."

OPPOSITE ABOVE RIGHT: The custom designed cabinetry in this study is finished in a distressed gold and platinum leaf to resemble the entablature frame of a fine Renaissance painting.

ABOVE: Solis Betancourt created a luxurious Adam-style backdrop in this light filled bathroom. A custom-designed vanity, marble and steel bench, and ceiling fixture bring richness to everyday activities.

SANDRA J. BISSELL INTERIORS

SANDRA J. BISSELL, ASID
337 SUMMER STREET
NORTH ANDOVER, MA 01845
(508)689-2360

PROJECTS:
Private Residences: Boston, the Andovers, Marblehead, Wenham, Wellesley and Milton, Massachusetts.

Commercial Work: Pediatric offices in Andover, Massachusetts.

CREDENTIALS:
ASID, Professional Member
Cornell University, BS
Syracuse University, Graduate Study
1993 First Place Winner, ASID National Design Competition
1993 Merit Award Winner, New England Chapter ASID

PUBLISHED IN:
The Boston Globe
The Boston Herald
Design Times
1001 Home Ideas

RIGHT: The serenity of the French blue and cream color scheme enriches the antique furnishings, among them a large gateleg oak table from the early 19th century.

PHILOSOPHY:
A room that looks as if it had evolved over time, gracefully accepting new acquisitions and beloved old possessions, furnishings that enhance rather than fight the architecture – this is the best of design.

My focus is on collaborating with my clients, interpreting their desires, incorporating their needs, and creating interiors that reflect their unique personal style.

Underscoring the esthetics of any interior design, must be an understanding of what makes a room comfortable and livable. Sensible space planning; proper use of scale, color, texture and pattern; attention to detail; and a generous infusion of creative ability elevates a room from the ordinary to the elegant, from trendy to timeless.

ABOVE: Effective lighting and custom-designed upholstery in rich tones of caramel, wheat, terra cotta and ebony complement the patina of the aged oak-paneled library walls.

LEFT: Fine paintings by Boston masters enhance the fireside seating area. The antique Georgian mahogany game table is graced by four classically inspired chairs faux painted to suggest satinwood, walnut burl and ebony.

Blair Design Associates, Inc.

DEBRA A. BLAIR
315 WEST 78TH STREET
NEW YORK, NY 10024
(212)595-0203 FAX(212)595-0245

PROJECTS:
Private Residences: New York; New Jersey; Connecticut; Massachusetts; Pennsylvania; Hawaii and Florida.

Commercial Work: Diamandis Communications, Inc., The Hearst Corporation/Avon Books, Regent Airlines, Fiduciary Insurance Company of America, Columbia Presbyterian Hospital Medical Offices, Maritime Overseas, Inc., Equitable Financial Companies, St. Regis Hotel and Donaldson, Lufkin & Jenrette, Inc.

CREDENTIALS:
ISID, Associate
West Chester University, B.F.A.
New York School of Interior Design
Fashion Institute of Technology
Bloomingdale's Design Staff, New York
Decorator Showcases: Mansions & Millionaires, 1983, 1985

PUBLISHED IN:
New Jersey Monthly Magazine
This Old House Kitchens
The New York Daily News
New York Newsday City Living
House Beautiful
Woman's Day
Woman's World
New York Magazine
Cosmopolitan
House Beautiful's Home Decorating
Residential Interiors
Working Woman

PHILOSOPHY:
The relationship established between client and designer is the most important aspect of interior design beyond pure aesthetic expertise. Good design doesn't just happen. Rather, it is a process that merges the uniqueness of the client with the designer's ability to interpret. More than a decade of experience has shown us that mutual commitment at the beginning makes for wonderful results in the end. Interiors should be more than just beautiful. They should be both inviting and functional, and the results should always be better than initially envisioned.

Zoya Bograd, Inc.

ZOYA BOGRAD
19 EAST 71ST STREET
NEW YORK, NY 10021
(212)734-8166 FAX (212)734-8168

OPPOSITE: In a most dramatic statement, the original Italianite interior of the hotel is enhanced with a newly commissioned ceiling painting of the four seasons, and the architectural detail is enlivened with a rich faux-wood finish and gilding. The superb proportions of the space now stand out, returning dignity and a delight in the arts to the establishment.

TOP RIGHT: An inviting tapestry painting of the Italian country-side greets guests at The Barbizon reception desk. Always decorated with flowers, this warm, wooded area projects a townhouse elegance for the renowned historic hotel, built in 1927 as a residence for women in the arts and now catering to an international clientele.

RIGHT: The club-like atmosphere of the hotel is reflected in this intimate lobby seating area, where tufted leather sofas mix comfortably with high-back chairs covered in a red stripe. The faux-marble table, which adds richness to the setting, was a salvaged piece transformed by hand-painted artistry.

ZOYA BOGRAD, INC.

PHILOSOPHY:
New York City - based Zoya Bograd, Inc. is a full-service firm that provides quality architectural and interior design services to hospitality, corporate and high-end residential clients.

Established in 1990, Zoya Bograd offers consistent service for large and small projects along with careful attention to detail. We pride ourselves on our ability to interpret the functional and aesthetic needs of each project in a creative, timely and cost-effective manner. Our approach is to bring out the individuality of clients, while enhancing the quality of their space and maximizing its use - the essence of successful design.

Our diverse design vocabulary permits us to cross from classical to modern design with equal versatility. Our proficiency in budget control and project supervision enables us to create new ideas while closely monitoring costs and keeping the completion date clearly in site.

ABOVE AND BELOW: The sweeping staircase, "a staircase to heaven" says some admirers, leads the eye up to a masterpiece ceiling fresco of the twelve signs of the zodiac, inspired by the Villa Farnese in Italy and executed by Russian artists under the designer's direction. The massive hexagonal columns have newly gilded capitols, adding to the sense of grandeur.

OPPOSITE: Among the touches of genius that carry out the celestial theme and contribute to an atmosphere of elegant dining are a custom chandelier, representing the sun with nine planets, and a painted tapestry of the moon.

MOËT

GEOFFREY N. BRADFIELD, JAY SPECTRE, INC.

GEOFFREY N. BRADFIELD, ASID
JAY SPECTRE, INC.
964 THIRD AVENUE
NEW YORK, NY 10022
(212)758-1773 FAX (212)688-1571

PROJECTS:
Private Residences: Mexico City; Toronto, Montreal and Calgary, Canada; Boston; Washington, D.C.; Houston; Dallas; Los Angeles; San Francisco; Chicago; the Hamptons and New York City, New York; Wichita, Kansas; Columbus, Ohio; Louisville, Kentucky; Palm Beach and Miami, Florida; Vail, Colorado; Tokyo; Okinawa; South Africa; Tel Aviv; France; London; several jets and a custom 120-foot yacht.

Commercial Work: Executive offices in New York; Washington, D.C.; San Francisco; Houston; Dallas; London; Mexico City; Wichita, Kansas and Louisville, Kentucky. Sculpture garden at the Art Gallery of Ontario.

CREDENTIALS:
Selborne College, A.A.
ASID
Author, "CELEBRATION Christmas in New York"
Co-author, "Point of View, Design by Jay Spectre"
Kips Bay Showhouse
The Metropolitan Home Showhouse
House Beautiful Showhouse
Tiffany & Company guest designer display

PUBLISHED IN:
Architectural Digest, 10/89, 7/90, 11/90, 12/91, 2/92, 12/92, 2/93
HG
House Beautiful
Habitat
New York Times
Metropolitan Home
Avenue
Who's Who In Interior Design

PHILOSOPHY:
Deeply rooted in the twentieth century, comfortably streamlined and yet ultra-glamorous. "I have always tried to align my work with forward looking concepts. Although I do not exploit this idea, it underlines my pro-technology spirit." "Functional opulence" is the key to the company's designs, incorporating fine antiques and high tech, and attaching the same sculptural value to utility objects as to important pieces of art. The result is superbly elegant, intensely comfortable environments that delight eye, mind and body alike.

RIGHT: An Ernest Feine painting suggests the panoramic views seen from this Manhattan apartment. The brushed steel and glass coffee and side tables were designed by Geoffrey Bradfield. The card table to the right was salvaged from the famed ocean liner The Queen Mary.

OPPOSITE: The mirror, glass and lacquer recessed vitrine showcases a collection of vases. The cabinet in exotic wood and inlaid ivory was originally commissioned for the Duke of Windsor's suite in The Waldorf Astoria Tower.

GEOFFREY N. BRADFIELD, JAY SPECTRE, INC.

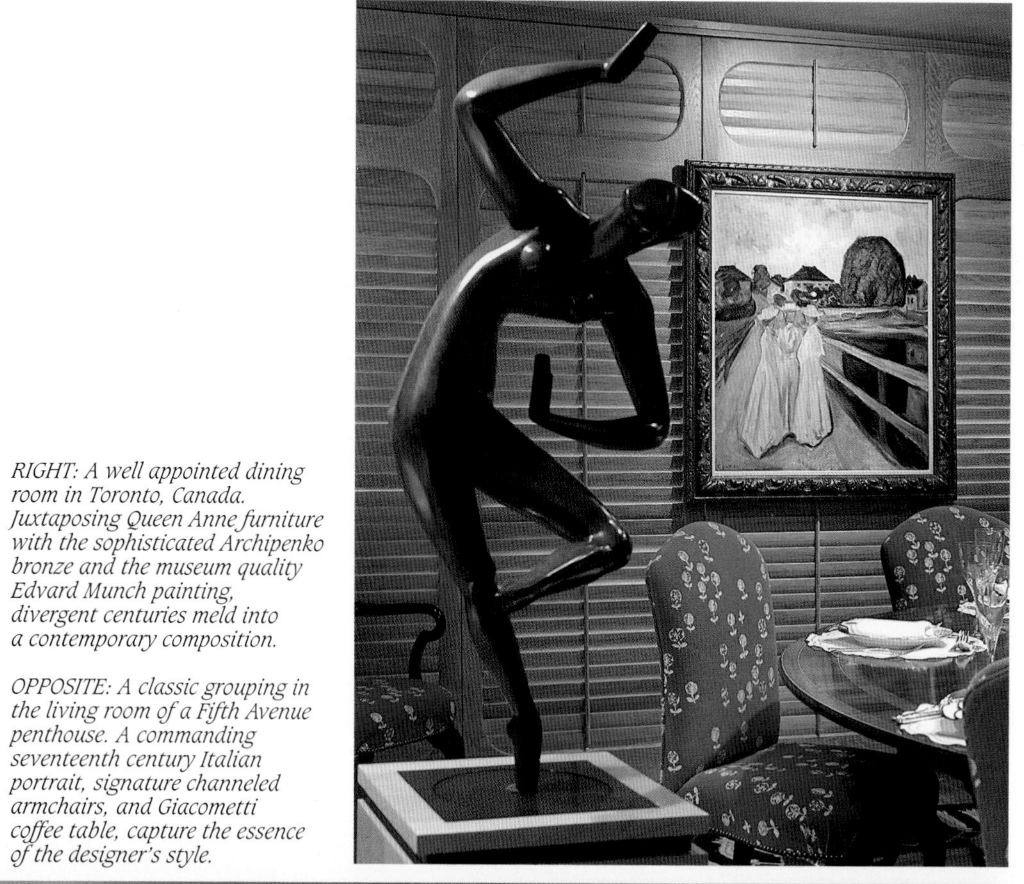

RIGHT: A well appointed dining room in Toronto, Canada. Juxtaposing Queen Anne furniture with the sophisticated Archipenko bronze and the museum quality Edvard Munch painting, divergent centuries meld into a contemporary composition.

OPPOSITE: A classic grouping in the living room of a Fifth Avenue penthouse. A commanding seventeenth century Italian portrait, signature channeled armchairs, and Giacometti coffee table, capture the essence of the designer's style.

BELOW: The library of a gentleman. Designed for a collector in Toronto, Canada, using rich exotic woods and lush upholstered mohair walls. Creating a sumptuous foil for the Edvard Munch drawings, Maillol bronzes and objets d'art.

THOMAS BRITT INC.

THOMAS BRITT
136 EAST 57TH STREET
NEW YORK, NY 10022
(212)752-9870

PROJECTS:
Private Residences: Mexico City; South America; India; Switzerland and throughout the United States.

CREDENTIALS:
Parsons School of Design
New York University, B.S.
ASID, Honorary Member
"Giant of Interior Decorating" Award, *Smithsonian Magazine*, 1987

PHILOSOPHY:
With residential and commercial projects worldwide, I design interiors ranging from contemporary to traditional, often creatively combining styles. Along with interiors, I also design furnishings that appear throughout my spaces.

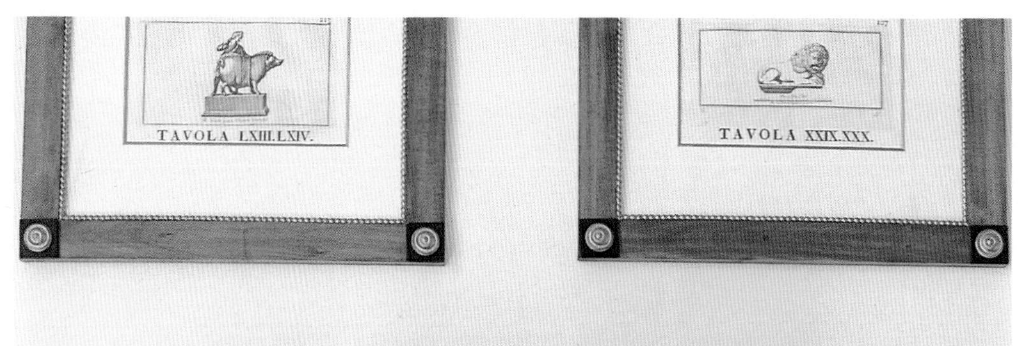

RIGHT: A Roman bust and antique engravings detail a living room that was a winner in House Beautiful's annual Showhouse Competition.

OPPOSITE: In the living room of the Edith Wharton Showhouse in Stockbridge, Massachusetts, designer Thomas Britt incorporated Latin phrases on the walls to welcome visitors.

THOMAS BRITT INC.

A former ballroom, now being used as a living room, features oversized sofas and 18th century chairs arranged on a bare parquet floor.

Mario Buatta Incorporated

MARIO BUATTA
120 EAST 80TH STREET
NEW YORK, NY 10021
(212)988-6811

PROJECTS:
Private Residences: Henry Ford II; Malcolm Forbes; Barbara Walters; Nelson Doubleday; Charlotte Ford and Billy Joel.

Commercial Work: Executive offices of the Metropolitan Opera House; Galleries of the Henry Francis DuPont Winterthur Museum and Blair House, The President's Guest House, Washington, D.C.

CREDENTIALS:
Member, Interior Design Magazine's Hall of Fame
Wagner College, Honorary Doctorate
Pratt Institute, Honorary Doctorate
Parsons School of Design, European Program
The Cooper Union–for Architecture Studies - Augustus Saint Gaudens Award
Historic House Trust, New York City, Board of Trustees
East Side House Settlement, Board of Trustees

PUBLISHED IN:
HG
Architectural Digest
House Beautiful
"W"
Town & Country
Vogue
English House and Garden
The New York Times Book of Design and Decoration
House and Garden Best in Decoration Book

LEFT: A dark leafy green background sets off this cool sitting room in a Victorian house in Connecticut. The tobacco leaf design chintz on the sofa is carried onto the windows (not shown). The tulip design rug from Stark Carpets grounds the client's collection of art and antiques.

ABOVE: Glazed pale lemon makes this San Francisco living room sunny even on the foggiest days. A smattering of Oriental floral chintz from Clarence House adds to the colors in the impressionist and contemporary paintings. The dhurrie carpet helps maintain a contemporary point of view, but the furnishings are a mix of traditional and modern styles.

LEFT: Lemon walls with off-white moldings frame a collection of porcelain floral plates and paintings. The simple dotted Swiss fabric works well with the pink plaid curtain and bed ensemble. The rose-patterned carpet sits on green-and-white bow carpeting (both from Stark). The oval mirror is English. The upholstery is designed by Mario Buatta for John Widdicomb Company and covered in fabrics from Brunschwig and Fils.

Mario Buatta Incorporated

LEFT: This canopied bed provides the perfect setting for an intimate and relaxing breakfast in bed. The color scheme uses a pleasing combination of blue-and-white chintz at the windows, a 19th century aqua birdcage, and touches of pale watermelon and green against lavender walls.

BELOW: The dark brown tortoise finish on the walls of this study creates a cozy and dramatic effect. The Portuguese chintz from Brunschwig & Fils on the upholstered pieces adds to the startling effect of pattern on pattern. Other strong notes are provided by the portrait over the sofa and the Goa (inlaid ivory) table in the forefront.

OPPOSITE: Selective use of primary colors creates a vibrant framework for the homeowner's extensive collection of fine paintings and porcelain. The screen lends an air of intimacy to the generously proportioned room, helping it serve as both a comfortable gathering place and an inviting retreat for enjoying a good book.

ANTHONY G. CATALFANO
71 NEWBURY STREET, SUITE 3
BOSTON, MA 02116
(617) 536-3776 FAX (617)536-9370

OPPOSITE: The two different levels of this room presented a challenge for designer Anthony Catalfano. Drapery treatments had to be very simple and mirror one another to reflect the additional height. Since there was not much room for furniture in the gallery area, Catalfano hung a collection of antique fish prints on the wall to add style. The use of Brunschwig and Fils upholstery makes the room rich and comfortable.

ABOVE: The overscaled moldings in this room made it a difficult space. The designer created the illusion of greater height by giving the room a pavilion effect through the application of a custom Brunschwig and Fils trellis wallpaper and border to the moldings, ceilings and walls. Drapery treatments were kept simple so as not to interfere with the views of the ocean. The room is used as a formal, yet comfortable, gathering place.

Anthony Catalfano Interiors, Inc.

PROJECTS:
Private Residences: Boston, Nantucket and Martha's Vineyard, Massachusetts; New York; Connecticut and Florida.

Commercial Work: Executive offices, restaurants, lobbies and corporate yachts.

CREDENTIALS:
12 years in interior design
References available upon request

PUBLISHED IN:
Palm Beach Illustrated
Design Times
Several New England publications

PHILOSOPHY:
As evidenced in the photographs of Anthony Catalfano's work, his unerring eye for detail and his commitment to his professional philosophy produce enduring results.

"Respecting the personal style and taste of each client, yet preserving integrity in my work, is a professional challenge that I enjoy," he says.

One of New England's most successful and respected young designers, Catalfano is known for the strength of his professional relationships with his clients and trade suppliers. He has worked with the same clients on different kinds of projects and believes that a strong relationship will produce satisfactory results throughout the years.

OPPOSITE: This room is a wonderful example of the detailing in a Boston brownstone. The 14 feet ceilings and 12 feet windows enabled the designer to make a strong statement with a black Clarence House floral linen print for the drapery treatments. The elegant flair of the room was accomplished by using the client's eclectic collections.

MARY W. DELANY INTERIOR DESIGN

MARY W. DELANY
ONE STRAWBERRY HILL COURT
STAMFORD, CT 06902
(203)348-6839 FAX (203)324-7229

PROJECTS:
Private Residences: Numerous private homes and apartments, including projects in Connecticut, New York, Pennsylvania, Florida, Colorado, Massachusetts and Canada.

Commercial Work: Mackintosh of New England headquarters, Boston; Cardiology Associates offices and waiting rooms, Darien and Stamford, Connecticut; Penn Central Energy Management Group, executive offices, Radnor, Pennsylvania; North American Bank, banking floor and executive offices, Waterbury, Connecticut; Moore McCormick Resources headquarters, Stamford, Connecticut; Collins Development model apartments, Greenwich, Connecticut.

CREDENTIALS:
Goucher College, B.F.A.
Junior League Showhouse, Fairfield, Connecticut, 1987, 1989

PUBLISHED IN:
Showcase of Interior Design, Eastern Edition, 1991
Fairpress
Connecticut Magazine
Table Settings, Knapp Press

PHILOSOPHY:
The firm's designs always respond to the client's needs and wishes and are directly related to the specific conditions and limitations of the building and its site. With an emphasis on comfort, each project is custom designed with attention to the smallest detail. The client's budget and time schedule are always observed closely. The end result should beautifully express the client's personality and lifestyle.

BELOW: A Chinese art deco rug provides a dramatic background for this mix of traditional and contemporary styles.

OPPOSITE: The recessed bar with black granite top and etched glass doors emphasizes the pale palette of this room.

Mary W. Delany Interior Design

OPPOSITE: Wicker, fossil stone and a hand-woven wool rug combine with nature to make this a sunny, pleasant family room.

BELOW: Gleaming silver, leather and polished granite create a special night drama in this dining room.

THE DESIGN OFFICE LTD. WELLINGTON HALL

FLORENCE KARASIK, ASID, PA, AIA
P.O. BOX 7330
SHREWSBURY, NJ 07702
(908)219-8700

CREDENTIALS:
ASID, Professional
AIA, Professional Affiliate
Illuminating Engineering Society
University of Chicago, M.A.
Brooklyn College, B.F.A., studied under Serge Chermayoff
Rutgers University, Post Baccalaureate

PUBLISHED IN:
HG
House and Garden Home Decorating Guide
Home Entertainment Quarterly
Robb Report
Country Accents
New Jersey Monthly Magazine
Goodlife
Garden State Home and Garden
Eclectic
Star-Ledger

PHILOSOPHY:
The architecture of a space and the client's wish list dominate my thoughts at the start of any project. The result: a multitude of design solutions ending in a look that is entirely relative to that project.

LEFT ABOVE: Island Heights, NJ, May 1993. Contempoary furnishings complement the 1910-era architecture.

LEFT: Nyack, NY, 1992. Sunny yellow helps a northeast-corner, tree-shaded bedroom come alive in the residence overlooking the Hudson River.

OPPOSITE: Lennox, MA, 1991. The music room is romantically recreated in a 1902 estate. Winner of the 1992 Residential Design of the Year Award from New Jersey Monthly Magazine.

D'Image Associates... Details & Design

71 EAST ALLENDALE ROAD
SADDLE RIVER, NJ 07458
(201)934-5420 FAX(201)934-5597

PROJECTS:
Private Residences: New York; New Jersey; Connecticut; Pennsylvania and Florida.

Commercial Work: Banks and executive offices in New Jersey and New York.

CREDENTIALS:
Fran Murphy:
ASID, Professional Member
NKBA, Certified Kitchen Designer

Laura Goomas:
ASID, Allied Member

Dorothy Bocchino:
ASID, Allied Member

Details & Design, gifts and accessories retail shop
French Designer Showcase
Nyack Showhouse
Mansion for Millionaires
National and state design award winners

PUBLISHED IN:
Better Homes & Gardens
Good Housekeeping
Kitchen and Baths
New Jersey Monthly
Garden State Home and Gardens
Woman's Day
New Jersey Good Life

PHILOSOPHY:
Each client's personality and lifestyle guides the design. Instinctive use of color, texture and architectural emphasis combine with visually enticing elements of contrast and detail to make our projects distinctive and beautiful. Combining the romantic with the whimsical is a hallmark of our work.

Through collaboration with the client, each design project is a sincere endeavor to fulfill expectations - regardless of budget limitations.

Details and Design, our furniture and accessories showroom, has become our greatest asset since it provides our clients with the opportunity to select objets d'art that express their individuality.

ABOVE: The great outdoors comes inside through this garden-room addition.

OPPOSITE ABOVE: A renovated kitchen results in a beautiful, functional space.

OPPOSITE BELOW: A custom glass, lucite and marble table enhances this elegant dining room.

D'IMAGE ASSOCIATES... DETAILS & DESIGN

LEFT: This bath features a 360-degree hand-painted tile mural depicting the Hudson River at the turn of the century - perfect considering the home itself was built in 1905 and overlooks the river.

BELOW: Wool tartans, antiques and overstuffed furniture give this gentleman's retreat a warm, cozy atmosphere.

OPPOSITE: Hand-woven silks and hand-painted panels help this small lady's boudoir capture the grandeur of time gone by.

Dixon Parker Design Group, Inc.

BARRY DARR DIXON, DESIGNER
R. ALBERT PARKER, BUSINESS MANAGER
4016 LINNEAN AVENUE NW
WASHINGTON, D.C. 20008
(202)537-4882 FAX (202)537-5036

L'Art de

Dixon Parker Design Group, Inc.

PROJECTS:
Private Residences: Washington, D.C.; Middleburg, Haymarket, McLean and Alexandria, Virginia; Bethany and Rehoboth, Delaware; Chevy Chase, Potomac, Bethesda, Annapolis and Baltimore, Maryland; Memphis, Tennessee; Jackson, Mississippi; Coconut Grove, Boca Raton and Palm Beach, Florida; New York City; Nantucket, Massachusetts and Jamaica.

Commercial Work: Washington, D.C.; Harriett Kassman Couture at the Willard Hotel, law offices of Tighe, Curhan and McInroy, model penthouse at Washington Harbour, offices of Newman and Hotzinger P.C., condominium lobby and model penthouse at 2401 Pennsylvania Avenue and Fifth Column Nightclub. McLean, Virginia: McLean Racquet Club, MSCI Corporation Headquarters and Courtside Bistro. Chevy Chase, Maryland: law offices of Muldoon, Murphy and Fawcette.

CREDENTIALS:
National Symphony Orchestra Showhouse, 1990-1993
University of Mississippi, B.F.A. Design, 1982 cum laude
Contributing writer: *Luxury Homes*
Guest speaker: various showrooms at the Washington Design Center
Guest designer: Washington Design Center "A Day With House Beautiful"

PUBLISHED IN:
Southern Accents, 1992, 1993, 1994
Better Homes and Gardens Decorating, cover, 1991
Washington Post, 1991, 1992, 1993
Style, cover 1993
Luxury Homes, 1993, 1994
Washingtonian Magazine
Metropolitan Home
Town and Country

PHILOSOPHY:
The integrity of good design is determined simply by what is "appropriate." Of course, the subjectivity of that word requires that clients align themselves with a designer who shares their vision.

To me, "appropriate" involves several levels of consideration. Architecture - what works well with the bones of a space - is paramount. Also important is transition, the thread that weaves its way through a home, simultaneously providing unity and flow and allowing diversion and interest. Comfort, even in the most formal areas, is mandatory, as is timelessness, a blessed attribute that straddles fad and period.

Quality involves both experience and knowledge. A good reproduction can be selected only with an understanding of the original. Balance and contrast involves many elements - color and texture, heavy and ethereal, old and new. One is as important as the other.

Successful design emanates a feeling, not just a look. Nuance is employed to fine tune the whole to the personality of the individual. In the best instances, the effect is a magical aesthetic harmony that is not initially surprising, at least not jolting. Upon inspection or reflection, however, the effect is cleverly unexpected.

Rodger Dobbel Interiors

RODGER F. DOBBEL
23 VISTA AVENUE
PIEDMONT, CA 94611
(510)654-6723

PROJECTS:
Private Residences: San Francisco and the surrounding Bay area; Palm Springs, Newport Beach, Los Angeles and Santa Monica, California; New York and New Jersey.

CREDENTIALS:
ASID
Chouinard Art Institute
Barron's Who's Who in Interior Design
Barron's Who's Who in Interior Design, International Edition
Marqui's Who's Who in the West
Marqui's Who's Who in the World
National Philantrophy Day Distinguished Volunteer Honoree Award, 1990

PUBLISHED IN:
House Beautiful
HG
HG, Kitchen and Bath
Better Homes & Gardens Decorating Ideas
Gourmet
Interior Design
Designers West

PHILOSOPHY:
It is through the magic created by the positive relationship between the client and the designer, plus the tools of light, color, texture and scale, that one can interpret creatively and have the sensitivity to reflect the lifestyle of the client. With the addition of quality workmanship, the attention to details and good business ethics, the end results can only be a relaxed elegance that reflects warmth, livability and luxury. Above all, the design project should be a pleasurable experience.

T. Keller Donovan, Inc.

T. KELLER DONOVAN
24 EAST 64TH STREET
NEW YORK, NY 10021
(212)759-4450 FAX(212)759-1242

PROJECTS:
Private Residences: New York City, East Hampton, Bridgehampton, West Hampton, Bedford, Locust Valley and Manhasset, New York; Short Hills, New Vernon, Summit and Livingston, New Jersey; San Francisco; Birmingham, Alabama; Vail, Colorado; Bermuda and Israel.

CREDENTIALS:
Bethany College, Bethany, West Virginia
Parsons School of Design, New York City
House Beautiful "10 Best Showhouse Rooms of 1985"
Kips Bay Decorator Showhouse Participant 1993

PUBLISHED IN:
"Manhattan Style" and *"Hampton Style"* by John Esten
"Making Space" by Sally Clark and Lois Perschetz
Architectural Digest
HG
House Beautiful
Glamour
Brides
Home
Country Living
Interior Design
New York Times
Chicago Tribune
Washington Post
Casa Claudia, Brazil

PHILOSOPHY:
Good design speaks for itself. Achieving that end requires creativity, innovation and resourcefulness, developing good client-designer relations and having a roster of talented crafts people to execute our ideas. Each project is very important to us because our satisfied clients are our best publicity.

TOP: "Kips Bay Decorator Showhouse - 1993"

Eberlein Design Consultants Ltd.

BARBARA EBERLEIN, ASID
1809 CYPRESS STREET
PHILADELPHIA, PA 19103
(215)732-0732 FAX (215)732-1210

LEFT: To emphasize the airy, outdoor character of this pastoral breakfast room, the flowing floral motif of the upholstery fabric was adapted as a floor stencil to suggest a charming area rug.

BELOW: Cool, aquatic themes recur throughout this beach-side residence, rendering the mood peaceful and the aesthetics powerful.

ABOVE OPPOSITE: Casual but substantial was the client's dream for this inviting terrace room, which embraces the natural beauty of the landscape.

BELOW OPPOSITE: His desire for bright, contemporary color was carefully melded with her penchant for antiques, and the result reflects this happy marriage of styles.

Eberlein Design Consultants Ltd.

BELOW: Arresting sapphire blue provides the foundation for a regal dining room where inlaid marble harmonizes with silver leaf and weathered metal.

OPPOSITE: A fine collection of 18th and early 19th century English antiques highlight the gilded quality of this sumptuous formal dining room.

PROJECTS:
Private Residences: Pennsylvania; New York; New Jersey; Delaware; Connecticut; Ohio and Washington, D.C.

Commercial Work: Historic restoration, museums, galleries, restaurants, retail stores, educational institutions, health-care, corporate offices, law firms, banks, government facilities, public spaces of residential buildings, hospitality and resorts.

CREDENTIALS:
Professional Member, ASID
Board of Directors, PA East Chapter ASID
Co-Chairman, Friends of Philadelphia Museum of Art
Board of Trustees, Rock School of Pennsylvania Ballet
University of Chicago, B.A. History
Faculty, University of the Arts, 1985-1989
Guest Critic, Moore College of Art, 1989-1994
Vassar Showhouse

Awards:
ASID Project Design Awards:
Historic Restoration
Contract, under 3,000 square feet
Residential, over 3,500 square feet
Singular Space, 2
Interiors Magazine:
Design in Philadelphia

PUBLISHED IN:
Interiors Magazine
Contract Design
1001 Home Ideas
Bride's
Redbook
Restaurant Design & Hospitality
Home Decorating Ideas
Philadelphia Magazine

PHILOSOPHY:
Founded in 1982, Eberlein Design Consultants Ltd. celebrates more than a decade of dedication to the creation of fine interiors.

Whether for renovations or new construction, displaying either traditional or contemporary detailing, Eberlein Design Consultants Ltd. has consistently produced a broad range of interiors that reflect the aesthetic tastes of the owners while maintaining meticulous attention to the technical appropriateness of materials and detail.

RIGHT: An intricately orchestrated palette and elaborate detailing conspired with English, French and Italian antiques to create a rich eclectic interior of distinct personality.

Nancy Eddy, Inc. Interior Decoration & Design

NANCY C. EDDY, ASID, ALLIED MEMBER
79 BATES STREET
DEDHAM, MA 02026
(617)329-0411 FAX (617)329-0411

PROJECTS:
Private Residences: San Francisco; Denver; Manhattan; Boston and Paris.

Commercial Work: Private offices, United Nations in New York and Boston law offices.

CREDENTIALS:
ASID, Allied Member
Mount Vernon College
Junior League of Boston Showhouse, 1991
Over 15 years of interior design experience

PUBLISHED IN:
Remarkable Private New York Residences
Boston Globe, Your Home Magazine
Design Times
This Old House Bathrooms, cover
Decorating
Woman's Day - Kitchen and Bath

Appearances:
Channel 4 news, NBC

PHILOSOPHY:
Classic design, whether traditional or contemporary, should be exciting and enjoyable, culminating in a heightened reflection of the client's taste and lifestyle.

A comfortable and inviting environment is achieved only through conscientious attention to detail and the utmost respect for the client's wishes, resulting in long lasting, collaborative client relationships.

ABOVE: An eclectic grouping of classic styles, combined with the pale color palette of the Aubusson rug, evokes a feeling of comfort and serenity.

OPPOSITE: A contemporary portrait hangs comfortably amid treasured heirlooms, its soft colors reflected in the room's furnishings.

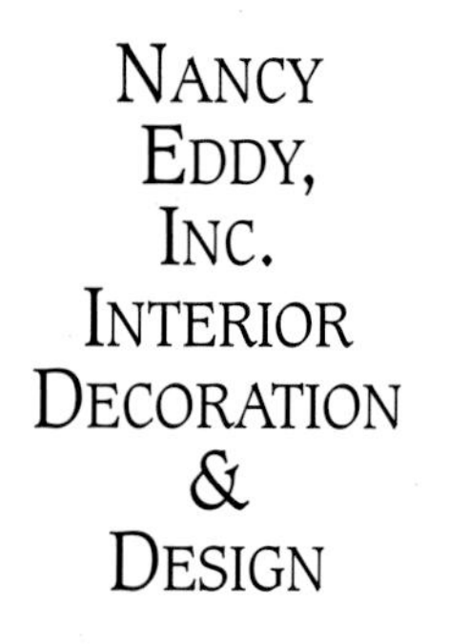

BELOW: Ceramic temple fruit and cottage roses sparkle in the glow of a handsome period alabaster lamp.

LEFT: Simple architectural lines and gleaming mahogany surfaces enhance this striking kitchen. Decorative walls reflect the owner's love of gardening, and a floral chandelier complements the effect.

BELOW: Warm terra-cotta shades, bold prints and whimsical accessories make this gentleman's room truly inviting.

Billy W. Francis Design/ Decoration, Inc.

BILLY W. FRANCIS
964 THIRD AVENUE, 11TH FLOOR
NEW YORK, NY 10155
(212)980-4151
FAX (212)980-4842

PROJECTS:
Private Residences: New York City and Bedford Hills, New York; Greenwich, Connecticut; Fisher Island, Florida and Houston, Texas.

Commercial Work: Greenway Bank & Trust; Boyer, Norton & Blair, Attorneys at Law.

CREDENTIALS:
ISID, Member
Interior Design Magazine Hall of Fame, 1988
Louisiana Technical University
The New York School of Interior Design
Barron's Who's Who in Interior Design
Architectural Digest - "AD 100," 1990
Kips Bay Showhouse, 1990

PUBLISHED IN:
Decorating Rich
Styled for Living
International Collection of Interior Design
Southern Interiors
Architectural Digest
Interior Design
House Beautiful
Southern Accents
Texas Homes
Home Magazine
Ultra
Town & Country

ABOVE RIGHT: This contemporary living room in a Houston home is warmed by French, Deco and Regency accents.

RIGHT: The dining room in this Brooklyn home is expansive enough to seat 22, yet cozy enough for an intimate gathering of four, thanks to a banquette built into the bay window.

OPPOSITE: A mixture of furniture styles bestows a feeling of understated elegance in the guest bedroom sitting area of the 1990 Kips Bay Showhouse.

Billy W. Francis Design/ Decoration, Inc.

RIGHT: Hand-stenciled walls in shades of beige help this large (40'x30') living room appear warm and comfortable.

BELOW: A rare combination of freshness and sophistication is achieved in this comfortable Ridgewood, New Jersey, living room.

OPPOSITE: This gleaming Houston townhouse features a clean, uncluttered style.

Gandy/ Peace, Inc.

CHARLES D. GANDY, FASID, IBD
3195 PACES FERRY PLACE NW
ATLANTA, GA 30305
(404)237-8681 FAX (404)237-6150

WILLIAM B. PEACE

BELOW: Texture is the key word in this comfortable, but subtle, informal living space. Diverse fabrics complement the sisal flooring and underscore the richness of the antique Chinese bamboo underwear, which is mounted on a custom cherry rod with bronze finials.

PROJECTS:
Private Residences: Atlanta; Cashiers, North Carolina; Fort Lauderdale and Naples, Florida; Chicago; Seattle; San Francisco; Washington, D.C.; Chattanooga and Knoxville, Tennessee; Tulsa, Oklahoma and Antigua, Guatemala.

Commercial Work:
Manufacturers' showrooms, restaurants, hotels and product design.

CREDENTIALS:
Recipient of many national and regional awards including:
National ASID Project Award, 1986, 1993
Southeast Designer of the Year, 1989, 1993, 1994

Charles D. Gandy:

Auburn University School of Architecture, B.I.D.
ASID, Fellow
ASID, National President, 1988
IBD

William B. Peace:

University of Kentucky, B.A.

PUBLISHED IN:
Southern Accents
Interior Design
Southern Living
Southern Homes
Atlanta Magazine
Design South
Designers West
Designers World
Atlanta Homes
Veranda
Interior Sources Magazine
Showcase of Interior Design, Southern Edition

PHILOSOPHY:
Capturing each individual client's spirit through simplicity, drama and classicism, we emphasize comfort and function in creating interiors that become canvasses for people, artwork and accessories through professional adeptness in lighting, detailing and creativity.

ABOVE LEFT: An antique Biedermeier secretary sits in contrast to an overscaled contemporary painting in this quiet and elegant living room. A pair of French chairs, upholstered in a delicate needlepoint, offer versatility by floating between two sitting groups.

LEFT: A subtle mix of damask against damask contrasts with the simplicity and strength of the deKooning drawings in this comfortable setting.

BELOW: Cherry paneling conceals file cabinets, books, computer equipment and other home office necessities in this beautiful yet functional library. The custom library cart provides easy access to reading material..

LEFT: A custom contemporary limestone fireplace pays homage to traditional details and serves as an anchor for the dramatic Bruce Brainard painting.

BELOW: The unifying elements of cherry and limestone create a "furniture" look for this round kitchen and adjacent family room. The down-filled banquette, cherry drink ledge, custom table(with one side open for remotes), and a collection of antique photos make this a warm and inviting center for relaxed living.

Sue Goldstein Designs, Inc.

SUE GOLDSTEIN-RUBEL
4321 MAIN STREET
PHILADELPHIA, PA 19127
(215)487-3337 FAX (215)487-9799

PROJECTS:
Private Residences: Center City Condominiums and Philadelphia Main Line area homes; Beach Homes: Longport and Margate, New Jersey; Winter homes: Fort Lauderdale, Delray Beach and West Palm Beach, Florida.

Commercial Work: Executive offices, KYW News TV and radio; private residential buildings, lobbies and common areas; Model homes and apartments for developers in Philadelphia and the New Jersey shore; professional offices for doctors, attorneys and restaurants; complete design and fabrications.

CREDENTIALS:
Moore College of Art
Sue Goldstein Designs, Inc. was created in 1963 as a full service design firm. The retail shop opened in 1986.
The New School
Individual courses in lighting, architectural rendering, photography
S.A.M. Award, Builders Association

PUBLISHED IN:
House & Garden
Philadelphia Magazine
Inside Magazine
Kitchen Design
Builders Publication
House Beautiful
Residential Interiors

PHILOSOPHY:
Timelessness is always my guide as I work to create environments that encourage growth, change and new thoughts. The bones of every project are space planning, textures and ambience. An intimate understanding of each client's needs, dreams and visions provides the foundation of my work.

TOP LEFT: Here, contemporary furnishings set off the traditional moldings and ceiling detail.

LEFT: Oversize natural fabric sofas invite guests to sit and enjoy a collection of African artifacts and artwork.

OPPOSITE: The gentle colors and rich textures in this timeless room provide an appropriate backdrop for the client's needlepoint pillows, art and accessories.

Sue Goldstein Designs, Inc.

LEFT: The shirred silk plaid fabric frames two windows and creates a backdrop not otherwise wide enough to hold the sofa. The oil painting above the sofa further establishes this as wall and not drape. The subtle colors showcase the collection of antique pieces.

BELOW: In this long, narrow room, the designer anchored the soft leather sofa and natural boulder cocktail table with an antique Kelim rug.

OPPOSITE: Strong pattern and color create an ambiance of warmth and conviviality in a family area that serves as the hub of the house. The print sofa provides a forgiving surface for family living.

Mark Hampton, Inc. Interior Design

MARK HAMPTON
654 MADISON AVENUE
NEW YORK, NY 10021
(212)753-4110

PROJECTS:
Private Residences: The White House, Blair House, The Naval Observatory (official residence of the United States vice president).

Commercial Work: The Metropolitan Museum of Art, Gracie Mansion and The National Academy of Design.

CREDENTIALS:
DePauw University
London School of Economics
New York University Institute of Fine Arts

PUBLISHED IN:
Mark Hampton on Decorating, author
Ledgendary Decorators of the 20th Century, author

PHILOSOPHY:
Decorating embraces people and beauty, peace and pleasure and the timeless activities of domestic life. A great love of architecture and the decorative arts, past and present, has been an important key to my design work. Many commissions result from my keen interest in restoration and preservation.

BELOW: The walls of a double-height Fifth Avenue drawing room overlooking Central Park are upholstered in wool damask. The room provides a powerful background for collections of books and objects d'art.

OPPOSITE: Another view of the Fifth Avenue drawing room shows custom-made bookcases filled with the client's collection of first editions on either side of an English marble mantel.

HEALING BARSANTI DESIGN & DECORATION

PATRICIA HEALING
239 MAIN STREET
WESTPORT, CT 06880
(203)222-0239 FAX (203)222-1239

DANIEL BARSANTI

PROJECTS:
Private Residences: Westport, Southport, Greenwich, New Canaan, Weston and West Redding, Connecticut; Oyster Bay, Muttontown, Great Neck and Manhattan, New York.

CREDENTIALS:
Patricia Healing:
New York School of Interior Design

Daniel Barsanti:
University of Bridgeport

HEALING
BARSANTI
DESIGN
&
DECORATION

Kenneth Hockin Interior Decoration Inc.

KENNETH HOCKIN, ASID
400 EAST 57TH STREET
NEW YORK, NY 10022
(212)308-6261 FAX(212)750-0537

PROJECTS:
Sutton Place, Park Avenue, Fifth Avenue, Central Park West, West End Avenue, Riverside Drive and other residences in New York City; Bronxville and East Hampton, New York; Greenwich, New Canaan and Wilton, Connecticut.

CREDENTIALS:
American Society of Interior Designers
NCIDQ
National Trust for Historic Preservation
Who's Who in Interior Design
International Institute of Interior Design
Monmouth College, B.A.
Junior League of Greenwich Showhouse
Friends of Thirteen Estate Showhouse
Kips Bay Decorator Showhouse

PUBLISHED IN:
British House & Garden
Traditional Home
House Beautiful's Home Decorating
The New York Times
The New York Times Magazine
Window Fashions
Victorian Decorating
Daily News
Ladies' Home Journal
McCall's
Furniture Today
Home Furnishings Daily
Classic Home

Books:
Showcase of Interior Design
Period Design and Furnishings
Interior Designer's Showcase of Color
Period Style
For Your Home: Bedrooms
Rooms With A View-Two Decades of Interior Design from the Kips Bay Decorator Show Houses

PHILOSOPHY:
I love color, and I understand it. I seek quality, and I know where to find it. I appreciate comfort, and I insist upon it. My clients tell me they love the rooms I create for them; I tell them I merely interpret their good taste.

William Hodgins

WILLIAM HODGINS, INC.
232 CLARENDON STREET
BOSTON, MA 02116
(617)262-9538 FAX (617)267-0534

BELOW: A personal collection of special objects, furniture and drawings fills a collector's room in Back Bay Boston.

OPPOSITE: A large, handsome mid-19th century bed made in the Caribbean, painted by Yorke Kennedy, lends scale and comfort to this bedroom. Books and flowers make this room a special retreat.

William Hodgins

RIGHT: Wide strip taffeta curtains and needlepoint roses surround a favorite dining chair.

BELOW: A Back Bay drawing room is furnished sparsely to capitalize on its light and airy appeal.

LEFT: Carefully placed between a pair of French doors, the desk for this home office almost seems to be in the garden.

BELOW: Simplicity and style are the hallmarks of this classic Palm Beach, Florida, dining room.

IDA Interior Design Applications, Inc.

IDA S. GOLDSTEIN, ASID
16 MUNNINGS DRIVE
SUDBURY, MA 01776
(508)443-3433 FAX (508)443-5251

PROJECTS:
Private Residences: Boston, New York and Palm Beach, Florida.

Commercial Work: Boston and New York.

CREDENTIALS:
ASID, Professional Member
Boston Design Center, Advisory Board Member
ASID New England, Vice President
Junior League of Boston Showhouses
"Best of Boston" Interior Designer, *Boston Magazine*, 1992

PUBLISHED IN:
Traditional Home
Better Homes and Gardens, cover
Design Times
Various Boston area publications

PHILOSOPHY:
Our efforts focus on creating interiors that best reflect the individual desires and needs of our clients. We spend time listening to our clients to obtain a better understanding of who they are.

Using proper space planning and architectural details as a base, we add light, color, form and accents to create beautiful and special homes.

ABOVE RIGHT: The reflection from a mirror frames a luxurious bedroom.

RIGHT: Works from various contemporary artists are combined to create a one-of-a-kind setting.

ABOVE OPPOSITE: Warm colors and contrasting textures help create a restful retreat.

BELOW OPPOSITE: Individually crafted furnishings contribute unique style to this relaxing room.

INTERIOR DESIGNS UNLIMITED

PATRICIA BONIS
8 FAIRWAY COURT
CRESSKILL, NJ 07626
(201)894-9082 FAX (201)894-1266

BASHA WHITE
4409 STANFORD STREET
CHEVY CHASE, MD 20815
(301)907-6786

PROJECTS:
Private Residences: New York City and Westchester, New York; New Jersey; Washington, D.C.; Maryland; Northern Virginia; Miami and Palm Beach, Florida.

Commercial Work: Law offices, Corporate Offices and model homes in Washington, D.C.

CREDENTIALS:
Patricia Bonis
Wellesley College, BA
Sorbonne, Paris, MA

Basha White
International Institute of Interior Design
ASID, Associate Member

PHILOSOPHY:
The most successful projects are the results of good communication between the client and the designer. We strive to design tasteful interiors that reflect the personality and aesthetic desires of our clients. With the benefit of experience and creative talent, our mission is to discern the timeless from the fleeting, to maximize the potential beauty and ...usefulness of every space.

OPPOSITE ABOVE: Color was an important factor in creating a 17th century atmosphere that enhances the Old Master paintings in the dining room of this newly built home.

OPPOSITE BELOW: Neutral colors and design simplicity blend with architectural highlights to set the mood for a tranquil master bedroom.

ABOVE: This elegant library, with its rich colors and woodwork, functions not only as the perfect setting for intimate entertaining by the fire, but also as a work area concealing extensive communications equipment.

CHRISTINE LAMBERT
912 FIFTH AVENUE, SUITE 3B
NEW YORK, NY 10021
(212)249-6939 FAX (212)472-6908

PROJECTS:
Private Residences: New York; London; Paris and Nice, France.

CREDENTIALS:
Parsons School of Design, New York
Sorbonne University, Paris, M.A.
Nice University, Nice, France, B. A.
French Designer Showhouse, New York, 1991, 1993
Interior Visions Showhouse and Gardens, Rye, New York, 1992
Saratoga Designer Showhouse, 1993

Associates:
UK: John Thornley, ARIBA
France: Anne Challamel

PUBLISHED IN:
The New York Times
Better Homes and Gardens-Window and Wall Ideas
House Beautiful

PHILOSOPHY:
My background explains my design style, which is eclectic to say the least. My design approach incorporates the formality of France, where I was born; the absurdity of England, where I worked for many years; and the anything-goes energy of America, where I now make my home.

A knack for creating harmony out of unlikely combinations of classical and eccentric elements is also obvious in my signature collages used as wallpapers and fabrics.

BELOW AND OPPOSITE: A tree-house bed made of pine bark frames a closet in the boy's room of this holiday house, leaving room for a large play area.

ROBIN HOOD

BELOW LEFT: The fabric and wallpaper, "Rhapsody in Sea Major," in this bathroom were custom designed and produced by Christine Lambert.

BELOW RIGHT: Gray flannel covers the walls of this elegant gentleman's dressing room.

BOTTOM: A collection of antique corkscrews displayed on wine crates adds interest to the wine cellar area.

OPPOSITE: A pleasant combination of French country antiques and a contemporary food-preparation area brings charm to a Manhattan kitchen.

Vivian Irvine Interiors

VIVIAN IRVINE
251 PARK ROAD
BURLINGAME, CA 94010
(415) 344-2634 FAX (415)344-2760

PROJECTS:
Private Residences: Hillsborough, San Francisco, Los Altos, Woodside, Atherton, Burlingame, Piedmont and San Mateo, California; Apartments in San Francisco and second homes in Lake Tahoe and Carmel, California.

Commercial Work: Retail shop and restaurant, Burlingame, California; waiting rooms and dental offices, Menlo Park, California and Coffee shop/bakeries, Sunnyvale/San Jose, California.

CREDENTIALS:
ASID, Allied Member
Rudolph Schaeffer School of Design
California State University
University of California Extension
Hillsborough Decorators Showhouse, ten years
House Beautiful, "Ten Best Designer Showhouse Rooms," 1987

PUBLISHED IN:
Attics & Basements, Ortho Books
Better Homes and Gardens, "Decorating," 1985 (cover) 1986, 1987,1988
Better Homes and Gardens, "Window & Wall Ideas", 1991
House Beautiful, 1987

COMPENSATION/FEE STRUCTURE:
Retainer, hourly fee, net plus percentage on purchases.

PHILOSOPHY:
To be an effective residential designer is to be a good listener. Clients' lifestyles and preferences give us the direction we need to design a project which is uniquely theirs.

Communication and honesty between designer and client are the vital elements to success. The atmosphere of trust cannot be overrated as this is more than a business - at its best, it gives pleasure to all parties involved.

With it's countless problems, this is at once satisfying, frustrating, challenging, exhusting, exhilarating, rewarding and at times, even a joyful experience.

Photos, above: John Vaughan; below: Jay Graham; photo opposite: John Vaughan

JAMES R. IRVING, ASID

JAMES R. IRVING, ASID
13901 SHAKER BOULEVARD
CLEVELAND, OH 44120
(216)283-1991 OR (216)751-1100

PHILOSOPHY:
My great passion is designing beautiful rooms. As a colorist-decorator, it is most important to capture the essence-persona of the client. Color and room arrangement are utmost. And I enjoy doing every last minute detail. My client list includes second and third generations of the same family.

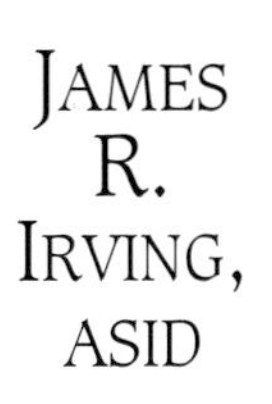

JAMES R. IRVING, ASID

PROJECTS:
Private Residences: Cleveland; Bermuda; Washington D.C.; New York; Chicago and Richmond, Virgina.

Commercial Work: Designer showhouses, corporate offices, country clubs and churches in the Cleveland area and throughout the United States and abroad.

CREDENTIALS:
ASID
Western Reserve University
New York School of Interior Design
Institute of Rome

Frederic Jochem Architectural Interiors

FREDERIC JOCHEM
240 CENTRAL PARK SOUTH
NEW YORK, NY 10019
(212)956-1840 FAX (212)956-1845

12 PASSAGE LANDRIEU
PARIS 75007 FRANCE
TEL/FAX: (1) 47 05 23 65

OPPOSITE: One of the client's requirements: to feature their eclectic collection while maintaining a sense of intimacy.

ABOVE: A luxuriously inviting living room in a "pied a terre" designed for a sophisticated European collector.

Frederic Jochem Architectural Interiors

PROJECTS:
Private Residences: In the U.S.A.: Manhattan, Washington D.C., Connecticut, New York State. In France: Paris and Provence.

Commercial Work: Lobby, Showroom, Professional offices, Antique Gallery, Retail Store.

CREDENTIALS:
University of Paris, B.A. in Law, Architecture and Fine Art, M.B.A. in Finance
New York School of Design
Established in 1989
French Designer Showhouse, New York, 1993

PUBLISHED IN:
House and Garden, October 1989, 1992
Harper's Bazaar, September 1991
The New York Times, March 1990, October 1993

Fee structure: Upon request.

PHILOSOPHY:
Our European approach to decorating is one of total collaboration with our client. The designer works to create for the client and his collection an environment which reflects the client's own taste, personality and intrigue. With a dynamic sense of serenity we invite the mind to be open and versatile, reflecting an unique and eclectic style of decorating.

Together the designer and the client achieve a dynamic mix, a tradition with a twist, which is characterized by a representation of many elements. All these elements, by their nature, texture and style, combine to create juxtapositions of fabrics, furniture, objects and paintings; juxtaposition of colors, shapes and scale; juxtaposition of periods, cultures and civilizations.

Properly executed by our skilled craftsmen and artisans, those innumerable elements, which define one's character, will reveal the interest, beauty and style of our clients and their unique sense of sophistication.

ABOVE LEFT: A detail of a bright, clean, contemporary, yet comfortable bedroom.

BELOW LEFT: Entrance hall gallery with classic architectural details for a contemporary art collection.

BELOW: A rendering to illustrate the extensive renovation that involves the construction of a balcony in a dining hall designed for grand entertaining.

Kerry Joyce Associates, Inc.

KERRY JOYCE ASSOCIATES, INC.
6114 SCENIC AVENUE
LOS ANGELES, CA 90068
(213)461-7808 FAX (213)461-3814

PROJECTS:
Private Residences: Interior architecture and interior design for residences in Los Angeles, Montecito, Newport Beach and Palm Springs, California and New York City.

Commercial Work: Store design; Restaurants; Corporate offices in Los Angeles and Palm Springs, California and Scottsdale, Arizona.

Product Design: Designer line of architectural fireplace mantels. Kerry Joyce furniture collection for James Jennings Antiques, Los Angeles.

CREDENTIALS:
Emmy Award for Set Decoration
New York University, B.F.A.
Society of Motion Picture & Television Art Directors
Metropolitan Homes "Design 100" issue, 1992, Featured as one of the top Interior Designers

PUBLISHED IN:
Angeles Magazine
Elle Decor
House & Garden
Los Angeles Times
Metropolitan Home

ABOVE: Cream and white beautifully set off a water gilded antique iron bed.

LEFT: Pale mint cabinet interiors set off an eccentric collection of whiteware.

OPPOSITE: Gold leafed dimensional wallpaper complement Regency inspired chairs.

Kerry Joyce Associates, Inc.

ABOVE OPPOSITE: Gentle colors harmonize a limestone checkerboard floor.

BELOW OPPOSITE: Granite and antiqued brass create a dramatic and handsome bathroom.

BELOW: The serenity of white showcases a tranquil grass garden.

PHILOSOPHY:
Kerry Joyce's interiors are characterized by a love for detail and fine materials. Able to work in a broad range of styles, he deftly creates satisfying interiors that reflect the personalities and lifestyles of his clients. "I love good design as well as comfort and I take it as a challenge to create an interior that will satisfy both." He believes strongly in the integration of architecture and interior design - having an affinity for both. "I reject trend or fad. Creating a timeless, enduring interior is very important to me."

KISER GUTLON ASSOCIATES, INC.

DANIEL J. KISER, ASID
29 EAST 10
NEW YORK, NY 10003
(212)505-7880 FAX(212)505-1226

PROJECTS:
Private Residences: New York City, Easthampton, and Long Island New York; Palm Beach, Boca Raton, Stuart and Naples, Florida; New Jersey and Connecticut.

Commercial Work: Executive offices in New York and West Palm Beach, Florida; country clubs in Long Island and Westchester, New York and West Palm Beach, Florida.

CREDENTIALS:
ASID, Professional Member
NCIDQ, Certified
Iowa State University, B.A.
Director of Corporate Interior Design, Bloomingdale's, New York
Director of Interior Design, Bloomingdale's, Garden City, New York
Chairman, Dean's Advisory Board, College of Design, Iowa State University

PUBLISHED IN:
Interior Design
The Designer
The New York Times
Palm Beach Life
Palm Beach Daily News
Woman's Day
Decorating Rich

The spectacular views from this 46th floor New York City apartment are complemented by mahogany cabinetry, Chinese Deco rugs, Oriental accessories and the client's fine art collection.

NEGRE
La Gomme
Félicien CHAMPSAUR

Kiser Gutlon Associates, Inc.

This Florida home provides a soaring atmosphere for large-scale Empire antiques, plush upholstery and period needlepoint carpets. The azure and creme scheme was inspired by the pool, brilliant sky and water beyond the boundaries of the living spaces.

T. L. Knisely Interiors

TERRY KNISELY
1911 EAST MARKET STREET
YORK, PA 17402
(717)757-2555 FAX(717)751-0704

EUGENE MONTGOMERY III

PROJECTS:
Private Residences: Pennsylvania; Maryland; Washington, D.C.; Virginia; New Jersey; New York; Florida; and South Carolina.

Commercial Work: Executive, legal and medical offices; restaurants; and country clubs.

CREDENTIALS:
Terry Knisely
Chicago School of Interior Design

Eugene Montgomery
George Washington University, BA

IFDA
"House Beautiful's Ten Best Showhouse Rooms," 1992
Duralee/Pugrant Showroom D&D Buildings, New York
Terry Knisely Fabric Collection through Duralee Fabrics, LTD.
Better Homes and Gardens National Showhouse, 1993
Various Showhouses on the East Coast
32 years of design experience

Photograph courtesy of *House Beautiful* copyright © October 1992. The Hearst Corporation. All rights reserved. Walter Smalling, Photographer.

PUBLISHED IN:
House Beautiful
Decorating
Better Homes and Gardens
Mid Atlantic
Baltimore Magazine
Style Magazine
Washington Post Magazine
Baltimore Sun
Luxury Homes

PHILOSOPHY:
Our design is based on the personality of our clients and the spirit of their homes. We employ quality furnishings and architectural sensibility to create harmonious and enduring interiors.

T.L.
Knisely
Interiors

Above: Meredith Magazine Decorator Showhouse 1993

Diane Alpern Kovacs, Interior Design, Inc.

DIANE ALPERN KOVACS
4 MAIN STREET
ROSLYN, NY 11576
(516)625-0703 FAX (516)625-8441

CREDENTIALS:
ASID, Allied Member
Syracuse University, B. A.
New York School of Interior Design
Parsons School of Design
House Beautiful Showhouse Award, Design Excellence
Guest Designer, Isabel O'Neil Foundation
Designers' Workshop

PUBLISHED IN:
HG
House Beautiful
Better Homes and Gardens Decorating
Country Home
Good Housekeeping
New York Times
Newsday
New York Daily News
Washington Post
Casa and Decoração, Portugal
Haven, Home Furnishings Council, cover

Books:
Mary Gilliatt's Decorating Book
Decorating For Comfort

Television Appearances:
Style With Elsa Klensch, CNN
The Home Show, ABC

PHILOSOPHY:
Since establishing my firm over two decades ago, I have gained recognition for my commitment to liveable design. A home or work environment should be defined by the people who use it, not vice versa. Responsiveness to a client's taste is my first consideration.

Although I handle a range of commercial and residential projects, I am probably best known for sophisticated country interiors. Clean lines, simplicity and finely wrought details give each project a unique stamp.

ABOVE OPPOSITE: The designer created a playful entrance by incorporating a hand-painted Parcheesi board on the floor.

BELOW OPPOSITE: A cozy library features a bold mix of patterns and textures.

ABOVE: An antique pine headboard, English chintzes and an heirloom quilt highlight this sunny bedroom.

Barbara Lazarus

BARBARA LAZARUS
10 FONES ALLEY
PROVIDENCE, RI 02906
(401)521-8910 FAX(401)438-8809

PROJECTS:
Private Residences: New York City and Westchester, New York; Short Hills, New Jersey; Boston and Stockbridge, Massachusetts; Hartford, Connecticut; Rhode Island; Palm Beach and Boca Raton, Florida.

Commercial Work: Country club, corporate executive offices, hotel lounge, professional offices and model homes.

CREDENTIALS:
Bennington College
Rhode Island School of Design
Newport Showhouse
Stockbridge Showhouse

Barbara Lazarus

PUBLISHED IN:
Decorating with Paper, Random House
Rhode Island Magazine
Providence Journal
Providence Journal Sunday Magazine, cover
Berkshire Eagle
Springfield Republican
Albany Times Union

PHILOSOPHY:
Good design is a professional guide, encouraging the client's own interests.

My projects might exude the rich comfort of a formal residence or the carefree casual feeling of a weekend retreat.

Ultimately, a designer should combine a client's aesthetic values and lifestyle to deliver a living environment that will endure.

Meadowbank Designs, Inc.

PENNY A. CHRISTIE
BOX 168
BRYN MAWR, PA 19010
(610)525-4909 FAX (610)525-3909

PROJECTS:
Private residences, clubs and executive offices in Pennsylvania, California, Florida, New Jersey, New York, Rhode Island, Virginia, Georgia, Washington, D.C., London and the Virgin Islands.

LEFT: An 18th century New York State chest in mahogany serves as the focal point of the dining room. A pair of Georgian candlestick lamps frame porcelain sculptures, and the original Edwards' prints portray a quartet of indigenous birds.

BELOW: Ceiling beams from an old barn, darkly stained wood blinds, an antiqued tile floor and blue cabinets recreate the look of a spacious Normandy farmhouse kitchen. In the background is a 19th century French, authentic signed Horloge tall case clock.

OPPOSITE: New construction is given the feeling of a 200-year-old manor house with the addition of a stone wall and beautifully oiled dark walnut floors. The French Bressane armoire in walnut burl and cherry, circa 1820, and beautiful Aubusson rug further this look of an age rich with tradition.

Meadowbank Designs, Inc.

PHILOSOPHY:
Every design project is a unique experience, a journey I share with my client. Meeting their expectations and fulfilling their trust is enormously satisfying.

The details of a home are critically important. A successful design must dovetail with the client's lifestyle and taste. Resolving problems of space, grand or small, is a welcome challenge, part of creating a rhythm in livable interiors.

Part of my professional role involves passing along information about art and art history - knowledge I gleaned from living in Europe and the Orient. I specialize in finding the right antique, one that can be appreciated by the client while appreciating in value. The greatest gratification of all is savoring the pleasure of a completed interior with a satisfied client.

LEFT: Quiet elegance, print on print, this medley of pattern and shape forms a perfect composition.

BELOW: A crisp country English setting is created in this historic Pennsylvania farmhouse. Antiques subtly fill the room, and color and pattern mix like old friends.

ABOVE OPPOSITE: Family photos and mementos help personalize the quiet sitting room retreat off the master bedroom.

BELOW OPPOSITE: Curved walls and dramatic window treatments help the spacious master bedroom seem almost enveloping. The massive French rope-twist poster bed reproduction is beautifully at home with the 18th century French walnut armoire.

David H. Mitchell & Associates

DAVID H. MITCHELL
1734 CONNECTICUT AVENUE NW
WASHINGTON, D.C. 20009
(202)797-0780

PROJECTS:
Private Residences: Washington, D.C.; Virginia; Maryland; Florida; Michigan; New York; Connecticut; Illinois and North Carolina.

COMMERCIAL WORK: Washington Harbor condominium lobby; Dakota Nightclub and Restaurant; Le Courtier of Washington; Metropolis Restaurant and Nightclub; Western Development executive offices; Warner Development and Barlet Company.

PUBLISHED IN:
Washington Post
Washington Post Sunday Magazine
House Beautiful Book on Color
House Beautiful
American Homestyle
Decorating & Remodeling
Southern Accents

PHILOSOPHY:
Our work is often perceived as modern, but we would rather not be pigeonholed into one style of design. We like to mix things up, using old with new, contemporary with antique and costly with inexpensive.

Our clients have a strong sense of individual style. As designers, our responsibility is to interpret and develop their ideas into a workable plan that reflects their personality.

David H. Mitchell & Associates

Juan Montoya

JUAN MONTOYA DESIGN CORPORATION
80 EIGHTH AVENUE
NEW YORK, NY 10011
(212)242-3622 FAX (212)242-3743

PROJECTS:
Private Residences: Worldwide experience, including homes of artist Fernando Botero and film producer Mario Kassar.

Commercial Work: Barney's apparel store, New York; Jones of New York showroom, New York and United Features Syndicate.

CREDENTIALS:
ASID, Professional Member
Parsons School of Design
Hexter Award for Interior of the Year, 1977, 1980
National Endowment for the Arts, Member
Interior Design Hall of Fame
Kips Bay Showhouse, 1979, 1987, 1992

PUBLISHED IN:
Architectural Digest
Arts & Antiques
Christian Science Monitor
Decoration International
Esquire
Gentleman's Quarterly
Home
House & Garden
House Beautiful
Interior Design
Interiors
Metropolitan Home
The New York Times
Southern Accents
Washington Post

LEFT: A dining area is created through the addition of a platform in the existing living area. A color palette of stone and turquoise is used to accent architectural details and lighten dark spaces.

BELOW: Through the careful manipulation of space and lighting, designer Juan Montoya achieves a sensitive balance between the functional needs of his client and the appropriate display of his client's extensive art collection.

OPPOSITE: Fabric wall hangings bring continuity to this two-story space, allowing for an intimate backdrop for the furniture around the fireplace. The fireplace, center table, chairs, pedestals and carpet were all designed by Juan Montoya.

Juan Montoya

RIGHT: Designer Juan Montoya evoked the spirit of the 1920s in his own New York apartment. His extensive art deco collection is exemplified in the French inlaid cabinet and silver vase in the background. The 19th century Italian stone vase and the 18th century Italian Rococo table are among the many eclectic objects displayed against this backdrop.

BELOW: An extensive remodeling project produced large public rooms that flow into one another to allow for flexible entertaining. The art deco-inspired furniture in the dining and living areas was designed by Juan Montoya.

ABOVE OPPOSITE: In this New York residence, a newly married couple gave the designer complete creative freedom, bringing only their art collection from their previous homes.

BELOW OPPOSITE: Evocative of the art deco luxury liners of the 1920s and '30s, this New York apartment extends its nautical feeling through expansive views to the East River.

CÉZANNE

CHARLOTTE MOSS & CO.

CHARLOTTE MOSS
16 EAST 65TH STREET
NEW YORK, NY 10021
(212)772-6244 FAX (212)734-7250

PROJECTS:
Private Residences: New York; Long Island; Connecticut; California; Colorado; Virginia; Delaware; Bermuda and St. Barts.

PUBLISHED IN:
HG
House Beautiful
Colonial Homes
British House and Garden
Town & Country
Los Angeles Times
Washington Post
The New York Times
Ville & Casali, Italy
Casa & Decoracão, Spain
W
Vogue

Appearances:
Style with Elsa
Klensch, CNN
Good Morning America
Lifetime Cable TV

PHILOSOPHY:
By emphasizing the basic elements of comfort and by balancing scale, color and detail, we create interiors that reflect the lifestyles of our clients. A strong collaborative relationship with our clients culminates in surroundings that are elegant, distinctive, personal and functional.

Charlotte Moss & Co.

MANHATTAN

VIONNET
BEATON IN VOGUE

Nile, Incorporated

TERESE CARPENTER
PATRICK NAGGAR
38 EAST 64TH STREET
NEW YORK, NY 10021
(212)688-8860

PROJECTS:
Private Residences: New York; Hobe Sound, Florida; Michigan and the Bahamas.

Commercial Work: Offices of Yves Saint Laurent, New York.

PUBLISHED IN:
HG
Elle Decor
The New York Times
Maison & Jardin

PHILOSOPHY:
The challenge of interior design is to meld the technologies of the future with those of the past, rich materials with those perceived as poor and simplicity with sophistication.

ABOVE: The sumptuous detailing of this collector's small library was inspired by design elements from ancient Greece.

OPPOSITE: A living space for serene contemplation created for a collector of objects from the 1920's.

BARBARA OSTROM ASSOCIATES, INC.

BARBARA OSTROM
ONE INTERNATIONAL BOULEVARD
MAHWAH, NJ 07495
(201)529-0444 FAX (201)529-0449

PROJECTS:
Private Residences: Clients throughout the United States and the Caribbean. Many prominent residences, including that of former President and Mrs. Richard Nixon.

CREDENTIALS:
ASID
New York University, B. A.
Pratt Institute, M. A.
The Sorbonne, Graduate Design Certificate
Kips Bay Boys & Girls Club Decorator Showhouse, 1985,1990, 1993
Hudson River Designer Showhouse, 1992
The Junior League of Greenwich Showhouse & Gardens, 1987,1991
Rogers Memorial Library Designer's Showhouse, 1987, 1989
Shrewsbury Designer Showhouse, 1988
Mansion in May, 1986, 1994
Named one of the top 50 design firms in the country by *House Beautiful*

PHILOSOPHY:
Barbara Ostrom Associates, Inc. is a nationally recognized interior design/ interior architecture firm. Founded by Barbara Ostrom in 1972, the firm does both residential and commercial design.

Before starting her own firm, Ostrom spent four years working with New York interior designer Roslyn Rosier, designing extravagantly elegant interiors for many distinguished clients, including the Duke and Duchess of Windsor and Aristotle Onassis.

In 1968, she was awarded the A.I.A. Award for Outstanding Architectural Achievement for the design of the North Star Mall in San Antonio.

BELOW AND OPPOSITE: A greenhouse "folly," abundant in architectural details and exotic furnishings. Built off site and hoisted to the 8th floor terrace of a New York City brownstone.

INTERIOR VISIONS
GREAT GARDENS OF BRITAIN Peter Coats

Barbara Ostrom Associates, Inc.

RIGHT AND BELOW: The grand living room of a Hudson River property projects designer Barbara Ostrom's ability to recreate period architecture, cabinetry, columns and mouldings while orchestrating color and texture, fabrics and furnishings, in a large scale setting.

LEFT: An odd shaped room lacking any architectural features was transformed into an eclectic retreat for a world traveler by the design and addition of arches, beams, corbels, and an antique French limestone fireplace. The awkwardly proportional window was enhanced into a focal point by the custom designed palladian arched shutter treatment.

BELOW: A stark New York City apartment suddenly came to life with the addition of unusual architectural treatments; Portuguese arches, beams, textured walls, reminding one of a fabulous country getaway in the south of France.

CAROL MELTZER
FOR P.T.M. INTERIORS UNLIMITED DESIGNS
107 EAST 60TH STREET
NEW YORK, NY 10022
(212)688-4430 FAX (212)688-4463

64345 VIA RISSO
PALM SPRINGS, CA 92262
TEL/FAX (619)322-6084

OPPOSITE: The deco inspired chandelier of mirror and chrome-plated steel was custom designed to compliment the Lalique dining room table.

LEFT: Featured from Carol Meltzer's product line is the "Aztec" Tablescope place setting.

BELOW: Custom tables by Carol Meltzer enhance the feeling of space that relies on the generous use of natural light.

P.T.M.
Interiors Unlimited Designs

BELOW: A bronze table designed by Carol Meltzer enhances the entrance to this "star-lit" living room.

PROJECTS:
Private Residences and Commercial Work: New York City and surrounding areas; Palm Beach, Florida; Los Angeles; Ontario; Tokyo and Osaka, Japan and London.

CREDENTIALS:
ASID, Accredited Associate Member
Screen Actors Guild
American Center for Design, Member
Fashion Institute of Technology
New York School of Interior Design
Association for International Color Directions

PUBLISHED IN:
The Designer
Glamour
The Daily News
The Daily News, "Suzy's Column"
The New York Times
Designer Showcases
Manhattan Magazine
House in The Hamptons
Who's Who in Interior Design, 1992, 1993, 1994
Center of Living, NY
Historic Preservation Lighting Seminar for ASID NY Chapter, Channel 13, News 12
Showcase of Interior Design, Pacific Edition, Eastern Edition

PHILOSOPHY:
Believing design is a reflection of life, I develop a total design concept for each project. My style focuses on harmony and nature and is combined with strong architectural lines. This balance creates a warm inviting atmosphere, which, coupled with art and antiquities, creates a new blend of tradition and a natural "environmental sense." I like my work to stand on its own, impervious to influences and passing trends.

ABOVE: "Star-lit" mirrored ceiling designed by Carol Meltzer.

Thomas Pheasant, Inc.

THOMAS PHEASANT
1029 33RD STREET, NW
WASHINGTON, DC 20007
(202)337-6596 FAX(202)342-3941

CREDENTIALS:
Registered Interior Designer
University of Maryland
Professional awards "Dossier Top Ten Best"
National Symphony Showhouse 1991, 1992
DIFFA - FXB House (Children with AIDS)

PROJECTS:
Private Residences: Washington, D.C. Metropolitan Area; Aspen, Colorado; Miami and Key West, Florida; New York; Jackson Hole, Wyoming and Caracas, Venezuela.

Commercial Work: Corporate, legal, executive and medical offices; art galleries; private clubs; various high-end retail shops; salons and boutiques.

PUBLISHED IN:
Southern Accents
Regardies
Stores
Metropolitan Home
Dossier
Home Magazine
Mid-Atlantic
Custom Home
The Washington Post
Housing Magazine
Washingtonian

OPPOSITE: Architectural details are reflected in custom ceiling design and antique gilt frames.

BELOW: Custom designed lyre base tables, armless chairs, sofa and ottoman by Thomas Pheasant, Inc.

THOMAS PHEASANT, INC.

PHILOSOPHY:
Thomas Pheasant, Inc., established in 1980, is an interior design firm involved in high end residential and commercial work. Each project is addressed individually, always aiming to create an aesthetically pleasing impression of suitability, quality and comfort.

Extraordinary attention is focused on the architectural details which define the character of the space and allows the selection of art work, antiques and collectibles to reflect the client's personality and set the spirit of the room.

RIGHT: Powder room/Private residence. Custom designed bronze bowl and vanity by Thomas Pheasant, Inc.

BELOW AND OPPOSITE: Custom designed folding screen, coffee table and woven metal nesting tables by Thomas Pheasant, Inc.

THE ITALIAN GARDEN
GIORGIO ARMANI
IMAGES OF MAN

Marian Potash Interiors, Inc.

MARIAN POTASH
29 BUTTONWOOD DRIVE
DIX HILLS, NY 11746
(516)462-6695

PROJECTS:
Private Residences: Long Island, Westchester, Rockland County, Queens and Manhattan, New York; New Jersey; Reston, Virginia; Dallas, Texas; Boca Raton and Fort Lauderdale, Florida.

Commercial Work: Executive offices in Long Island and Manhattan, New York and Fort Lee, New Jersey.

CREDENTIALS:
ASID, Allied Member
Long Island University, B.S.
Parsons School of Design
Seven Designer Showhouses

PUBLISHED IN:
House Magazine, Lifestyle of the Island, 1993
New York Times Home Section, 1991
Unique Homes, 1989
Kitchen and Bath Concepts, 1988, 1989
The Designer, 1988
Nevamare Decorative Surfaces Advertising Brochures

ABOVE RIGHT: Audio and media components are incorporated smoothly into this comfortable den. Careful use of accessories softens the overall effect.

RIGHT: The challenge here was to make a small space both functional and architecturally interesting. New walls support a custom lacquered desk top and shelving.

OPPOSITE: Plenty of storage space was a prerequisite for this Long Island dining room. The custom ebony ash unit with granite top functions as both a server and storage cabinet.

Gayle Reynolds Design

GAYLE REYNOLDS, ASID
7 FESSENDEN WAY
LEXINGTON, MA 02173
(617)863-5169 FAX (617)863-1104

PROJECTS:
Private Residences: Texas; St. Louis and the Boston area.

Commercial Work: Corporate Management Offices, doctor's office, and Corporate Realtors Offices.

CREDENTIALS:
Maryville Collage, BFA Cum Laude, Interior Design and Art History
ASID, Professional Member
Junior League of Boston Decorators' Show House and Garden Tour 1987, 1992, 1993

PUBLISHED IN:
Boston Globe
Window Fashions
Design Times

PHILOSOPHY:
My clients come to me with personality, style, and preferences. My job is to inspire them in new and imaginative ways. As a result of my years of experience, I am able to offer my clients extensive resources, quality creative design, project coordination, and professionalism down to the last detail.

I want my clients to feel relaxed and secure when they work with me. Their environments should meet their rational and emotional needs. Finally, I want them to have a unique sensory experience every time they enter a space we've created together.

LEFT: A personal library makes a classic statement about a homeowner. This one is tucked away in a corner of the family room.

OPPOSITE TOP : A cozy conversation area at the end of a long, narrow living room provides relaxed comfort for social gatherings.

OPPOSITE BOTTOM: This third floor guest suite combines comfortable California upholstery with Old World elegance. The soft colors and textures are emotionally soothing.

DONALD A. RICH
23 WEST PUTNAM AVENUE
GREENWICH, CT 06830
(203)661-6470

PROJECTS:
Private Residences: Greenwich, Connecticut; New York; Florida; Pittsburgh, Pennsylvania and Washington, D.C.

Commercial Work: Corporate offices in New York and Greenwich, Connecticut.

CREDENTIALS:
New York School of Interior Design

PHILOSOPHY:
I establish a close working relationship with my clients by encouraging their input in the design process. My goal is to achieve a timeless, understated look by combining antiques with comfortable upholstery. Furthermore, I feel that carefully integrated accessories are an essential element of all successful rooms.

OPPOSITE: Traditional and transitional pieces combine to bring an aura of refined comfort to the living room in a Greenwich, Connecticut, home.

DONALD A. RICH INTERIORS & ANTIQUES

ABOVE: Elegant furnishings greet guests with a traditional welcome in this foyer.

RIGHT: Furniture placement creates an intimate area in an otherwise panoramic living room.

Pedro Rodriguez Interiors Residential/ Commercial

PEDRO RODRIGUEZ, FASID
2215 LOCUST STREET
PHILADELPHIA, PA 19103
(215)561-3884 (215)567-5378

MARGATE, NJ
(609)822-9512

PROJECTS:
Private Residences: Philadelphia and Eastern Pennsylvania; New York; New Jersey; Florida and Washington, D.C.

Commercial Work: Professional and corporate offices, restaurants, model homes and condominium public spaces.

CREDENTIALS:
FASID, Fellow American Society of Interior Design
American Design Institute, Havana
New York School of Interior Design
Designer of Distinction Award, PA East Chapter, ASID
Many national and local distinguished service citations, ASID
Designers Choice Award, RNS Cancer Research Fund Showhouse
Participated in Vassar Scholarship Fund Showhouse since 1973
PDIAF Showhouse to benefit AIDS
PA East Chapter ASID Showhouse

PUBLISHED IN:
House Beautiful
Home Decorating
Philadelphia Magazine
Philadelphia Inquirer
Philadelphia Bulletin
Atlantic City Press
Miami Herald
The Designer
Norristown News
Atlantic City Magazine
Burlington Times
Courier Post
Custom Homes
Who's Who in Interior Design

PHILOSOPHY:
I am proud to say that I have received the ultimate compliment. In the 25 years since the founding of Pedro Rodriguez Interiors, I have been called upon by former clients to refresh past projects or to design new homes.

In many cases, I have been retained by a second generation of clients to provide the thoughtful, versatile, thorough and creative services that have become my hallmark.

Pedro Rodriguez Interiors Residential/ Commercial

John F. Saladino, Inc.

JOHN F. SALADINO
305 EAST 63RD STREET
NEW YORK, NY 10021
(212)752-2440

PROJECTS:
Private Residences: Los Angeles and Montecito, California; New York, Amagansett and Great Neck, New York; Atlanta; Denver; Deal, New Jersey; Palm Beach and Williams Island, Florida; Jackson Hole, Wyoming and Boston.

Commercial Work: Nutrasweet; Chase Manhattan Private Banking; Almay; Boscobel Hotel, Jamaica; Lilian Vernon and Homestead Inn, Greenwich, Connecticut.

CREDENTIALS:
University of Notre Dame, B.F.A.
Yale University, School of Art and Architecture, M.F.A.
Parsons School of Design, Board of Directors
Steuben Glass, Board of Directors
Save Venice, Board of Directors
Daphne, 1985, Award for Design Excellence in Dining Room Furniture
Interior Design Magazine Hall of Fame, Charter Member, 1985
Chicago Design Fest Award for Excellence, Residential Design, 1983
Euster Merchandise Mart Award for Outstanding Leadership in the Field of Interior Design, 1982
The Chicago Design Sources Committee First Annual Award in Residential Design Excellence, 1982

PUBLISHED IN:
Architectural Digest
Architectural Digest 100
House Beautiful
HG
Metropolitan Home
Taxi
Vogue Decoration
Interior Design

TOP LEFT: Built on a hill in Montecito, California, this house draws its inspiration from Vignola's 16th century Villa Farnese outside Rome. Designer John Saladino has restored the house to its original splendor.

LEFT: Trompe l'oeil murals depict the view from an Italian loggia. The sycamore and lacquer table is a Saladino design.

OPPOSITE: Rich wood paneling establishes a mood of history and discovery in this distinguished library.

Justine Sancho Interior Design, Ltd.

JUSTINE SANCHO, ASID, IFDA
1106 CHURCHVIEW PLACE
ROCKVILLE, MD 20854
(301)340-8605

4909 CORDELL AVENUE
BETHESDA, MD 20814
(301)718-8041 FAX (301)718-8305

PROJECTS:
Private Residences: Maryland; District of Columbia; Virginia; New York; Connecticut and California.

CREDENTIALS:
ASID, Professional Member
IFDA
University of Maryland

PUBLISHED IN:
Southern Accents
Luxury Homes
Style
The World & I
Potomac Life

LEFT: In this alcove, special attention was paid to keeping sight lines open to the antique harp and music stand.

BELOW: An understated elegance is achieved by mixing antique, traditional, and contemporary pieces.

Justine Sancho Interior Design, Ltd.

PHILOSOPHY:
My firm is dedicated to customer satisfaction. I collect each client's thoughts and tastes, stretch their imagination, and then create for them a comfortable, timeless interior. I take advantage of a wide selection of home furnishings, including antiques and custom-designed pieces, to bring uniqueness and variety to each project.

Close communication, patience, and attention to detail are my trademarks. I work closely with clients to clarify objectives and set priorities. This collaboration helps clients avoid costly mistakes and stay focused on creating exciting interiors that enhance their lifestyle.

OPPOSITE: Antiques, trompe l'oeil stonework and contemporary furnishings help create an indoor/outdoor environment.

Cesar Lucian Scaff, Inc.

CESAR L. SCAFF, ASID
ROBERT M. KRYCH, ASID
KRIS M. KOCHER, ASID

9 NANTUCKET COURT
BEACHWOOD, OH 44122
(216)831-2033

777 BAYSHORE DRIVE
FORT LAUDERDALE, FL 33304
(305)561-5588

OPPOSITE: The elevator foyer in this Boca Raton, Florida, apartment features a sculpture by Trova.

ABOVE: Furnishings from both the 18th and 19th centuries lend an air of grace and comfort to this living room.

RIGHT: The courtyard of designer Cesar Scaff's house in southern Florida.

BELOW: A 19th century pine console and Venetian blackamoor serve as focal points for this entry hall.

OPPOSITE: A George II console and an old Venetian painting (attributed to Jacabo Bassano) introduce a generous helping of dining elegance.

BOLLA
Cesar
Grazie lla

Janet Schirn Design Group, Inc.

JANET SCHIRN, FASID

541 FIFTH AVENUE
NEW YORK, NY 10175
(212)682-5844

401 NORTH FRANKLIN
CHICAGO, IL 60610
(312)222-0017

821 DELAWARE AVENUE, SW
WASHINGTON, D.C. 20024
(202)554-0017

PROJECTS:
Private Residences: United States; Great Britain and France.

Commercial Work: Adler Planetarium, Ann Klein, Brunswick Corporation, Chicago White Sox, Georgetown University, Goodyear, Holly Hunt, M&M Club, Masland, Metropolitan Structures, St. Charles Manufacturing and Tootsie Roll.

CREDENTIALS:
ASID, Fellow, Past National President
AIA, Professional Affiliate
International Federation of Interior Architects/Designers, Executive Board
Pratt Institute, B.F.A
Columbia University, M.F.A
University of Illinois, Architecture

AWARDS:
ASID National Honor Award
Midwest Honor Awards
Illinois Designer of the Year Award
Halo Lighting Competition Honor Awards
Chicago Lighting Institute Honor Awards
Who's Who
Who's Who in Interior Design
Eastman-Kodak/PPA Honor Award
Merchandise Mart Distinguished Designer Award
ASID National Residential First Prize Award, 1993

PUBLICATIONS:
Major consumer shelter and trade publications world-wide
Textbooks
Janet Bailey, *Chicago Houses,* St. Martin's Press, NY

PHILOSOPHY:
Creativity...sophistication...comfort... classicism...timelessness...individuality... characterize our work. Architectural orientation, lighting and art are important to it.

Excellent design, whether cutting-edge or traditional, is our goal. As is excellent service, whether individual or corporation. Client needs, objectives and attitudes are reflected in each project, creating highly individual personal expressions.

Sylvia Schulman Interior Design, Ltd.

SYLVIA SCHULMAN, ISID
RONI GILDEN, ISID ASSOCIATE
203 LAKESIDE DRIVE SOUTH
LAWRENCE, NY 11559
(516)239-0362 FAX (516)239-3147

10082 SPYGLASS WAY
BOCA RATON, FL 33498
(407)482-6144

ABOVE: Raspberry lacquered walls and silk fabric add to the drama of this dining room vignette.

ABOVE OPPOSITE: Informal dining at its best. A plaid skirted table with printed pleats along the bottom sets the stage for this breakfast room where relaxation is of the essence.

OPPOSITE BELOW: Chenille sofas, wool plaid pillows and poof, leopard velvet bench and wool ribbed carpeting all add warmth to this contemporary den. The strength of the sun pouring through the French doors and windows makes you want to curl up and read a book.

PROJECTS:
Private Residences: New York metropolitan area, Long Island and Westchester, New York; Florida; Connecticut; Tucson, Arizona; Vail, Colorado; Berkshire, Massachusetts and Jerusalem.

Commercial Work: Corporate, legal, financial, medical and dental offices and a funeral home.

CREDENTIALS:
Sylvia Schulman

Participated in eleven showhouses
ISID
Traphagen
F.I.T.
New York School of Interior Design

Roni Gilden

ISID Associate
Ohio State University
Hofstra University

PUBLISHED IN:
HG
House Beautiful
Architectural Digest
W
The New York Times
Windows and Worlds
Interior Design Magazine
Home
Home Entertainment
Newsday

PHILOSOPHY:
A home is a reflection of people and their particular lifestyle. It is our philosophy as designers to help our clients create an ambiance that they can feel comfortable in on a daily basis.

Color, pattern and styling is viewed personally and it is our responsibility to bring these elements together along with liveable pricing in order to satisfy our clients' aesthetic and financial needs.

Through professional business practices and empathy as "people first" we develop a rapport with our clients which makes a potentially difficult period of time run smoothly. We treat each project with a sense of humor, respect for people, attention to detail and an emphasis on reality.

This combination results in "success" for all!

Lait pur
Stérilis
Quillot frères

Sylvia Schulman Interior Design, Ltd.

ABOVE OPPOSITE: Plaid wool walls contrast with crisp white antique linens to set the mood in this sophisticated bedroom based on the Provence region of France. The Steinlein poster is an outstanding example of French antique poster art.

BELOW OPPOSITE: This bedroom sitting area is enhanced with Portuguese fireplace tiles, needlepoint rug and trompe l'oeil shutters. The portrait over the original mantel adds a touch of whimsy.

BELOW: Toile walls and fabric combine with wide-striped window treatments to create a dining room that is both soft and striking. The rock crystal chandelier illuminates the skirted table with inverted pleats. The overall effect is formal, yet not stuffy.

SHIELDS & COMPANY INTERIORS

GAIL SHIELDS-MILLER
43 EAST 78TH STREET
NEW YORK, NY 10021
(212)794-4455 FAX(212)794-3881

PROJECTS:
Private Residences: New York City, Westchester, Long Island, the Hamptons, Fire Island and Shelter Island, New York; Connecticut; New Jersey; Miami, Boca Raton and Palm Beach, Florida and the Bahamas.

Commercial Work: Residential buildings, model apartments and homes in New York; professional offices, retail businesses and industrial facilities in New York and Connecticut.

CREDENTIALS:
ASID, Allied Practitioner
Adelphi University, B.A., M.S.
Parsons School of Design

PUBLISHED IN:
IDH/Interior Decorators Handbook
Avenue
House
Woman's Day
Spotlight
New York Magazine
North Shore Magazine
Home Entertainment
Good Living

Photo: David Sabal

PHILOSOPHY:
Successful design combines four elements: the client, the designer, taste and exceptional craftsmanship. The creative juxtaposition of these elements adds up to unbeatable elegance and style.

Whether a traditional or contemporary home is desired, the designer must interpret the needs of the client by personalizing and customizing various design elements. A designer must know how to balance both the ornate with the plain, the old with the new, to achieve a sense of timelessness.

ABOVE OPPOSITE: Glass block, high-tech lighting and a "sculpted" ceiling provide a sense of openness to this windowless kitchen.

BELOW OPPOSITE: Art Deco style furnishings enhance the backlit "slice" in the stepped wall of the stairway.

LEFT: Shades of taupe, steel grey and lipstick red complement the zebrawood paneled bar.

BELOW: The stainless steel and brass cocktail table floats before the sofa, camouflaging the original division between an outdoor terrace and the interior of a New York City apartment.

Photo: Davis Sabal

PASSION BY DESIGN
FOLK ART
ART DECO INTERIORS

Shields & Company Interiors

OPPOSITE: This dramatic great room takes on an added dimension through the use of hand-painted wall panels. TV and stereo equipment are concealed in the antique armoire.

LEFT: Hand-carved Italian candlesticks, a matte black porcelain vase and a Hilde Cayne painting complement the traditional elements of this room.

BELOW: The brass and wrought-iron railing and the mahogany bar with gold-leaf detailing were both custom-designed.

STEBBINS & CO.

CINDY STEBBINS
79 EAST PUTNAM AVENUE
GREENWICH, CT 06830
(203)661-0066 FAX(203)661-0881

PROJECTS:
Private Residences: New York; Greenwich, Connecticut; Fort Worth, Texas; Nantucket, Massachusetts; Wilmington, Delaware: Del Ray, Florida.

Commercial Work:"Yvonnes" at Locke-Ober, Boston; "Skybar", Clarke Cook House, Newport, Rhode Island and Tommy Hilfiger Corporate Offices, New York.

CREDENTIALS:
Rhode Island School of Design,
University of Copenhagen
Greenwich Showhouse
1992 Interior Visions, Rye, New York

PUBLISHED IN:
House Beautiful
Woman's Day, Bed and Bath Ideas
Greenwich Magazine
Greenwich Times
Woman's Day, "W"
Decorating Ideas

PHILOSOPHY: Stebbins & Co. strives to create interiors that are timeless, elegant and appropriate.

JOHN STEDILA
TIM BUTTON
175 WEST 93RD STREET
NEW YORK, NY 10025
(212)865-6611 FAX(212)865-5021

PROJECTS:
Private Residences: Client list upon request.

Commercial Work: Louis; Boston; Botticelli; Perry Ellis; Paul Stuart; Leslie Fay Company; Belle France; Endicott Bookseller; Bank of Argentina; Sofi; Enoteca.

PUBLISHED IN:
Biedermier
Interior Design
Interiors
Elle Decor
Private Palm Beach
Metropolitan Home
House Beautiful
New York Magazine
New York Times Magazine, Sunday Edition
Arts and Antiques
Passion for Detail

Stedila Design, Inc.

TOP: Clean lines, soft textures, and a simple color palette create a sense of peace in this New York penthouse.

BELOW: One of Addison Mizner's 1922 oceanfront mansions, this Palm Beach, Florida, residence features an addition that's historically accurate but furnished for today's lifestyle.

RIGHT: The Kips Bay Showhouse in New York boasts an atelier bridge of steel and aluminum grille, accessed by hidden stairs behind the cracked-plaster wall. Indicative of the Stedila Design style is the mixture of classic furnishings with contemporary materials and architectural details.

Stedila Design, Inc.

PHILOSOPHY:
A sense of timeless style, a fastidious attention to detail, and a commitment to creating highly personalized spaces in which to live or work — these are the hallmarks of Stedila Design, Inc.

RIGHT AND BELOW: A golden master suite, spare yet elegant, serves as an inviting private retreat in this Palm Beach, Florida., home.

LEFT: An opulent salon ideal for entertaining in the grand tradition.

BELOW: A renovated barn has been transformed into a casual retreat for a New York family.

KAREN SUGARMAN INTERIORS

KAREN SUGARMAN
185 NORTH MAIN STREET
ANDOVER, MA 01810
(508)475-2930 FAX(508)475-9030

PROJECTS:
Private Residences: Massachusetts, Maine, New Hampshire, Rhode Island, Florida and Louisiana.

Commercial Work: Medical and legal offices.

CREDENTIALS:
ASID, Allied Member
Northeast Louisiana University, B.S.
Swampscott Showhouse 1986, 1988
York Decorators' Showhouse 1990
Junior League of Boston Showhouse 1991, 1992, 1993
Window Fashions Design Award 1990

PUBLISHED IN:
Better Homes and Gardens Window and Walls (Cover)
Better Homes and Gardens Bedrooms and Baths (Cover)
1001 Home Ideas
Design Times
Boston Globe
Boston Herald

PHILOSOPHY:
The relationship between designer and client should be a partnership where ideas can be freely exchanged. The designer should pay careful attention not only to what the client is saying, but also to the subtle cues that emerge during their collaboration. The result of these exchanges should be a room with ambience and charm unique to each client's personality.

OPPOSITE ABOVE: An opulent silk window treatment harmonizes with a cherished heirloom rug to create an image of gracious old world dining.

OPPOSITE BELOW: A sophisticated living room, perfect for entertaining or intimate gatherings, overlooks the twinkling lights of Boston Harbor.

ABOVE: The whimsical teapot fabric and fanciful teapot chandelier welcome the family to a sunny breakfast even on a dismal day.

ANNE TARASOFF INTERIORS

ANNE TARASOFF, ISID
25 ANDOVER ROAD
PORT WASHINGTON, NY 11050
(516)944-8913 FAX (516)944-7256

PROJECTS:
Private Residences: New York City, Southampton, Nassau County and Westchester County, New York; Boston; Franklin Lakes, New Jersey; Greenwich, Connecticut; Williams Island, Key Largo and Jupiter, Florida; Acapulco, Mexico; Calamatra, Greece; Washington, D.C. and Bethesda, Maryland.

Commercial Work: Law, medical and corporate offices.

PHILOSOPHY:
My approach to design is based on the integration of the client's lifestyle with a visual harmony embracing uncontrived comfort.

I love to create romantic rooms that have an understated elegance. This is achieved with imaginative use of color, pattern and detail.

PUBLISHED IN:
House Beautiful
House and Garden
The New York Times
New York Newsday
Interior Decorators Handbook, cover
Colonial Homes
Better Homes & Gardens
New York Magazine
The Designer
Who's Who in Interior Design
Interior Visions
Home in the Hamptons, cover
Unique Homes
Woman's Day
Windows & Walls
Westchester Illustrated
Kitchen & Bath Concepts
House
Home Decorating

Anne Tarasoff Interiors

ANNE MARGARET BAUM
VILLAGE GREEN
BEDFORD, NY 10506
(914)234-3071 FAX (914)234-0540

PROJECTS:
Private Residences: Westchester County, New York and Fairfield County, Connecticut; New York; Cape Cod, Maine and Palm Beach, Florida.

CREDENTIALS:
Allied Board of Trade, New York School of Interior Design
1992 Interior Visions Showcase and Gardens
1991 Junior League of Greenwich Showcase House
1990 Greenwich Garden Guild Showcase

PHILOSOPHY:
The clients of Trilogy require surroundings that are appropriate, timeless, practical and elegant. Each interior we design reflects the tastes of the owners and is achieved by careful attention to detail and consideration of lifestyle choices. Our objective is to create an environment that combines the needs of the client with the skill of the professional interior design firm to provide carefully planned solutions to design needs.

Right: Sunshine pours into this attractive niche, complementing the grand yellow silk curtains.

Below: The oversize living room of this residence has as its focus the magnificent formal gardens beyond the large bay window.

Opposite: This library, formerly a garage, serves as the informal gathering place for a large family.

VIORICA BELCIC
424 MADISON AVENUE
NEW YORK, NY 10017
(212) 222-2551 FAX (212) 222-2201

BELOW: Walls, ceilings, moldings and columns form a background against which the best of the old is combined with the best of the new.

OPPOSITE: Timeless elegance fills the living room of this 6,000 square foot New York apartment that had been gutted prior to renovation.

PROJECTS:
Private Residences: New York, Long Island and the Hamptons, New York; Greenwich, Connecticut; Montreal and Paris.

Commercial Work: Hambro-America Inc., European Tax Network, Grant Thornton, Lincoln Savings Bank, Cullman Ventures, CBS Songs, Ladenberg Thalmann, Commonwealth Secretariat and Chicago Research & Trading.

CREDENTIALS:
AIA
ASID, Allied Member

PUBLISHED IN:
The New York Times
Metropolitan Home
Unique Homes
Vogue International
Bath Design

PHILOSOPHY:
Being careful never to compromise my professionalism, my goal is to carry out the wishes of my clients while gently steering them toward choices of quality and taste.

ABOVE: Client, designer, architect and contractor worked together to complete a complex project on time and within budget.

LEFT: Contemporary luxury is the hallmark of this Bridge Hampton, New York, residence.

OPPOSITE: Here, a young girl is able to play, read and fantasize in a cozy loft-type bed surrounded by treasured belongings.

Visconti And Company, Ltd. Designed By Vince Lattuca, ISID

VINCE LATTUCA, ISID
245 EAST 57TH STREET
NEW YORK, NY 10022
(212)758-2720

PROJECTS:
Private Residences: Throughout the United States and Europe.

Commercial Work: Tropic Tex International, and lobbies of San Remo in New York.

CREDENTIALS:
ISID, New York Chapter
ISID, former Vice President and International Representative, New York Chapter
Parsons School of Design, Educator
Commendation Awards in Resources Council Product Design Competition, 1983, 1989
Deco Preservation Society

PUBLISHED IN:
The New York Times
HG
Home Entertainment
House Beautiful
French Vogue
Interior Design
New York Magazine
Town & Country
Interior Visions/Great American Designers
Showcase of Interior Design, Eastern Edition I, II

PHILOSOPHY:
Education is the key to good design. I define it as the ability to take a client's dreams and transform them into their reality.

Every project should spring from a constant dialogue between designer and client so that the ultimate success belongs to both. A designer's work should always reflect quality and great attention to detail.

Visconti And Company, Ltd. Designed By Vince Lattuca, ISID

OPPOSITE: Room designed in collaboration with Judi Schwarz, ISID.

THE GARDENS OF JAPAN
ART DECO EVA WEBER

WEIXLER, PETERSON & LUZI

STEVEN ANTHONY WEIXLER
WALTER BAYARD PETERSON
MARCELLO LUZI, ASID
2031 LOCUST STREET
PHILADELPHIA, PA 19103
(215)854-0391

PROJECTS:
Private Residences: Philadelphia; New York; Boston; Washington, D.C.; Seattle; San Francisco; Charleston, South Carolina; Palm Beach, Jupiter Island and Miami, Florida; Bogota, Columbia; and Ascoli Piceno, Italy.

Commercial Work: Dunn Capital Management, Inc.; Connecticut National Bank; PNC Financial; Pennsylvania Real Estate Investment Trust; Shawmut National Trust Company.

CREDENTIALS:
Licensed Interior Designers
NCIDQ Certified
American Society of Interior Designers
Philadelphia Athenaeum Associates
Philadelphia Design Industry AIDS Fund Showhouse, 1989
Vassar College Scholarship Fund Showhouse, 1986, 1987
Zurbrugg Hospital Designers' Showhouse, 1988

OPPOSITE: An exceptional 12-panel Coromandel screen provides a dramatic backdrop to the custom designed furnishings created especially to accommodate a tall husband and petite wife in their living room.

ABOVE RIGHT: Robin Daniel's canvas, "Red Untitled," hangs on a chimneybreast of Florida coquina stone. Cabinets contain antique Chinese objects. "Patinated Compotier," a sand-cast glass bowl by California artist John Lewis, rests upon a lacquered chinoiserie low table from Christopher Norman, Inc.

RIGHT: In this bedroom, seen from the pool terrace through fully opened glass doors, the designers used subtle textures and quiet colors to enhance a sense of intimacy.

Weixler, Peterson & Luzi

PUBLISHED IN:
Who's Who in Interior Design, International Edition
Interior Visions: Great American Designers
House Beautiful
Florida Designers Quarterly
Philadelphia Magazine

PHILOSOPHY:
With backgrounds in architecture, design and the decorative arts, Weixler, Peterson and Luzi was established in 1981 to address the special needs of prestigious residential and commercial clients who seek highly personal attention to detail. Such attention promotes a dialogue between client and designer that results in spatial relationships and design elements which better serve a client's needs.

Weixler, Peterson and Luzi insist that "the role of a good decorator is to vanish." Their work, which has earned them national recognition, covers a broad stylistic range. The firm is frequently selected by clients who want the design of their homes to reflect their lives and enhance their interests.

LEFT: In the foyer, viewed through the living room, city lights reflect in a mirror above a Joseph Meeks card table and a Rosa Bonheur bronze. To the left, above a curved loveseat in Bergamo velvet, hangs a French Apostolic Palace scene by Bernard Borione from Frank S. Schwarz & Son. "Byron's Pool on the Granta" by Joseph Murray Ince (English, 1880) is on the right wall.

OPPOSITE: Under festoon curtains of Clarence House silk taffeta, a pair of Portuguese Louis XV fauteuils surround a Regency writing table from Kentshire. Bouillotte lamp is from Kensington Place Antiques; antique silver from Niederkorn. On the mantel sit three pieces of delft from Bardith. Oil painting above and watercolors to the left are from Frank S. Schwarz & Son.

BELOW: A Smith of Chichester landscape over the sofa and near an English Regency table balances a rare George III Scottish wing chair and a Philadelphia secretary opposite. Traditional proportions in the contemporary cocktail table complement a pair of Louis XV giltwood fauteuils. The walls are overglazed and varnished to achieve a subtle backdrop.

LOUISVILLE

John Robert Wiltgen Design, Inc.

JOHN ROBERT WILTGEN, ISID
300 WEST GRAND AVENUE
CHICAGO, IL 60610
(312)744-1151

PHILOSOPHY:
The integration of art, architecture and design is what makes our homes timeless.

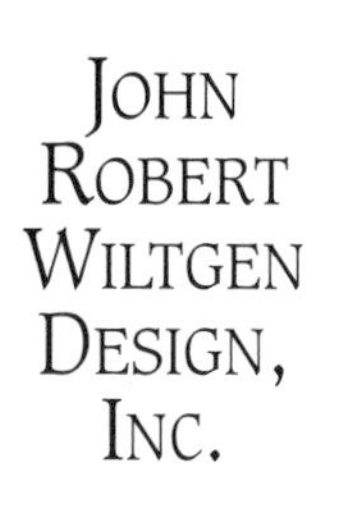

John Robert Wiltgen Design, Inc.

Index Of Interior Designers

INDEX OF PHOTOGRAPHERS